Leadership in Libraries

CHANDOS
INFORMATION PROFESSIONAL SERIES

Series Editor: Ruth Rikowski
(email: Rikowskigr@aol.com)

Chandos' new series of books is aimed at the busy information professional. They have been specially commissioned to provide the reader with an authoritative view of current thinking. They are designed to provide easy-to-read and (most importantly) practical coverage of topics that are of interest to librarians and other information professionals. If you would like a full listing of current and forthcoming titles, please visit www.chandospublishing.com or email wp@woodheadpublishing.com or telephone +44 (0) 1223 499140.

New authors: we are always pleased to receive ideas for new titles; if you would like to write a book for Chandos, please contact Dr Glyn Jones on email gjones@chandospublishing.com or telephone number +44 (0) 1993 848726.

Bulk orders: some organisations buy a number of copies of our books. If you are interested in doing this, we would be pleased to discuss a discount. Please contact on email wp@woodheadpublishing.com or telephone +44 (0) 1223 499140.

Leadership in Libraries

A focus on ethnic-minority librarians

MAHA KUMARAN

CP
CHANDOS
PUBLISHING

Oxford Cambridge New Delhi

Chandos Publishing
Hexagon House
Avenue 4
Station Lane
Witney
Oxford OX28 4BN
UK
Tel: +44 (0) 1993 848726
Email: info@chandospublishing.com
www.chandospublishing.com

Chandos Publishing is an imprint of Woodhead Publishing Limited

Woodhead Publishing Limited
80 High Street
Sawston, Cambridge CB22 3HJ
UK
Tel: +44 (0) 1223 499140
Fax: +44 (0) 1223 832819
www.woodheadpublishing.com

First published in 2012

ISBN:
978-1-84334-658-6 (print)
978-1-78063-308-4 (online)

Typeset by Domex e-Data Pvt. Ltd.
Printed in the UK and USA.

Dedicated to my amma and appa
A. R. Srinivasan (late)
and
S. Premavathi

Contents

List of figures and tables

Figures

Tables

List of abbreviations

ABS	Australian Bureau of Statistics
ACRL	Association of College and Research Libraries
ACS	Australian Computer Society
ALA	American Library Association
ALIA	Australian Library and Information Association
ALISA	Australian Library and Information Science Abstracts
ALJ	Australian Library Journal
APALA	Asian Pacific American Library Association
ARL	Association of Research Libraries
ASLA	Australian School Library Association
BMAT	Biomedical Admissions Test
CILIP	Chartered Institute of Library and Information Professionals
CLA	Canadian Library Association
EI	Emotional intelligence
ESEA	Elementary and Secondary Education Act (of 1965)
GMAT	Graduate Management Admission Test
GRE	Graduate Record Examination

IELTS   International English Language Testing System

LCDP   Leadership and Career Development Program

PLA   Public Libraries Australia

SAT   Scholarly Aptitude Test

SPL   Saskatoon Public Library

TOEFL Test of English as a Foreign Language

Foreword

Library and leadership are two words that we often hear in the context of the future of libraries. Regardless if you are attending a conference, participating on a webinar, attending training, or even listening to a guest lecturer, we hear about the multi-layered leadership challenges libraries, of all types, are facing. Are we, the library profession, in a leadership crisis? If so, how will we prepare, select, and place future leaders that represent a diverse society that is ever changing? Maha Kumaran has taken a bold leap to offer her thoughts through this book, *Leadership in Libraries*, with its focus on ethnic and immigrant minorities. When we think of ethnic minorities, we use a privileged Western-centered definition that focuses solely on race. Kumaran's work documents the needs of immigrant librarians and how other countries consider their backgrounds, regardless of race, as ethnic minorities. This text offers advice to those immigrant librarians who are interested in library leadership by offering tips on communication, transitions, cultural norms, and cultural differences (such as the value placed on time, for example). The advice given addresses the idiosyncrasies that exist in libraries, in the West, and will help prepare and develop immigrant librarians who may consider a leadership role in the future. This advice will not only prepare the immigrant librarian, it will also provide guidance for managers who want to motivate immigrant librarians to pursue a leadership role in the library.

Leadership theories are amongst the vast pool of knowledge in the literature. Maha provides an overview of leadership theories and connects them to the needs of immigrant librarians. Though the various leadership theories and training programs exist, there is still an urgent need to prepare and recruit future leaders from diverse backgrounds and immigrant librarians are another group that will add diversity in the library profession. As the world continues to develop globally, and our cultural borders blend, libraries should encourage immigrant librarians to help fill the leadership gap. Maha describes the issue of race and the tensions facing countries that have historical issues, and provides examples of such historical tensions when discussing the election of President Barack Obama. "To the world watching, what was obvious during this election campaign was that it is not easy for a visible minority to assume a leadership role in a country where the majority of the population is white." This same sentiment could be true for visible minorities leading organizations that are, like the US, predominately white. Regardless if it is race, language, and/ or religion, and the issues surrounding diversity are the same in every country. "While there are some commonalities of this concept of leadership among various countries, there are differences as well."

This book will help immigrant librarians, who are transitioning into a new culture, to adapt to a new environment and as Maha states, "emerging leaders should not take adversity and conflict personally." *Leadership in Libraries* will encourage the embracing of differences while sharing the comprehensive needs for immigrant librarians. There is so much more in this volume that will aid managers, leaders, supervisors, and librarians alike. Maha has taken care to provide a well-rounded approach towards motivation, understanding needs, skills development, and styles. This book will add value to the vast collection of leadership literature by adding a unique voice and reflection on immigrant and ethnic-minority librarians and their journey to become leaders.

Jerome Offord, Jr
Assistant Professor, Dean of Library Services and University Archives
Head, Department of Library and Information Science
Lincoln University
Missouri, USA

December 2011

Acknowledgements

Just as a leader cannot come into existence without the support of many around him or her, this book would not have seen the light of day without help from my family, colleagues, my editors and my publisher.

A big thank you to my editors, Jonathan Davis and Geraldine Lyons, for their help every step of the way in the development of this book. They were very patient as I dealt with personal life issues along the way. I would also like to thank Glyn Jones from Chandos Publishing for finding me and asking me to write a book on leadership. I would not have considered writing a book on anything this soon in my career if you hadn't asked me.

I would like to thank my previous employer, the Saskatoon Public Library, for giving me the opportunity to take part in my very first Leadership Development Program that was the inspiration for this book. I would like to thank my current Dean, Dr Vicki Williamson at the University Library, University of Saskatchewan, for giving me the opportunity to attend the Library Leadership Development Program and for creating the intellectual atmosphere that enabled me to write this book.

Thanks also to Sara Mueller, Research Facilitator, University of Saskatchewan, for assisting me with my survey questions and research grant application; my colleague, Christine Neilson, who took the time to read my initial drafts and offered valuable advice and comments; and to my research assistant, Amol Ghorpade, for putting together all the figures and tables and for his assistance with the survey software.

I would also like to thank all survey participants, library organization leaders and staff, and many others who answered my questions along the way and contributed to different aspects of this work.

Sincere thanks are also due to Jerome Offord, the Dean of Library Services and University Archives at Lincoln University, Missouri. Despite his busy schedule, he graciously accepted my invitation to read my book and offer his thoughts in a foreword. Who better to write a foreword to this subject than Jerome who has served as the Diversity Officer and Corporate Inclusion Manager at OCLC, the Director of Diversity Initiatives with the Association of Research Libraries, and penned various articles on diversity in the library workforce?

Last but not least, I want to thank my boys: my husband, my very first mentor and best friend, for putting up with my mental and physical absences while I was working on this book and for his moral support throughout this project; and our delightful boy who is now 11 years old and still can't believe his mom wrote a whole book. Neither can I. Keep working on your story Magizh (James Kumaran) and you will soon have a book too!

Mahalakshmi Kumaran
December 2011

About the author

I am the older of two daughters born to middle-class parents in India. Education and results from school performance were important; extra-curricular activities were not part of our lives.

I moved to Canada with my husband in 1994. I had no intention of becoming a librarian. I had finished my MA in English and my M.Phil. course (not the thesis) when I moved here. The Canadian economy in the 1990s was doing so badly that I had a hard time getting even dishwashing jobs. I felt lucky when one of the part-time jobs I landed was at a branch of the Saskatoon Public Library (SPL) as a page. I worked close to 15 hours a week for about $5 an hour – it was back-breaking, repetitive work and the pay was poor, but I enjoyed being in a library setting. From here I moved on to other positions within the library and later worked in three other libraries across Canada. Since I always worked as a library assistant, when I had the chance I decided to go to library school and get a degree in library science. Again I was lucky to be hired by SPL as their Adult and Young Adult Librarian for almost two years and then Virtual Reference Librarian for over two years. After this I moved to the University of Saskatchewan, an academic library.

I did not become a librarian until 2005, which is when I graduated – not because I was not interested, but due to many personal circumstances. My eventual aim had been to go to library school, which I did, but until then I was just another immigrant struggling to find my way in my new home and any thoughts of leadership didn't occur to me. And it is only recently, after my first leadership exposure through SPL, that I became interested in the concept. There are many minority immigrants like me from different professions who either have not considered leadership as a possibility for them or who think of leadership as unattainable in their new land. I hope this book will inspire them to consider leadership positions in their organizations. Personally, I know I still have ways to go ... and that there is more to learn. As the Tamil saying goes: கற்றது கைமண் அளவு கல்லாதது உலகளவு (What you have learnt can fit into your palm, what you haven't is as big as the universe).

Mahalakshmi Kumaran
December 2011

Introduction

Abstract: Canada, Australia, the UK, and the US have a considerable number of minority immigrants and many more continue to move there. The social make-up of these immigrants has changed from earlier times – there are more from Asia, Africa, and the Middle-East moving to these countries. These immigrants, in spite of their education and experience from their home countries, often have a difficult time finding jobs and settling in, let alone trying to be leaders in their field. They need help in securing a place in the community, finding a job that they are trained for, and then becoming leaders in their organization. This is minority leadership and it is different from cross-cultural leadership. There are also differences between a first generation immigrant minority leader and leaders from the second or third generation immigrant population. While the last two identify themselves with what is their native culture, first generation immigrants are still torn between their native culture and the new culture in which they live. This may not be true of all immigrant minorities – some seek and find opportunities and flourish quickly, others take a long time, and many just focus on their children's futures.

Key words: minority leaders, minority leadership, cross-cultural leadership, visible minorities, minority leadership literature, Australia, UK, United States, Canada, diversity

In the fall of 2009, when I was still the Virtual Reference Librarian at the Saskatoon Public Library (SPL) in Saskatoon, Saskatchewan, Canada, I had the opportunity to attend the

Leadership Development Program organized by the City, funded by my employer (for me) and offered through the Edwards School of Business, University of Saskatchewan. It was an eight-week session (one evening a week) covering a range of topics from Understanding Leadership, Emotional Intelligence, Encouraging the Heart, and being a role model as a leader. The program was taught by various facilitators and attended by people from various job fields – a physician, a soup-kitchen manager, police officer, manager of a senior home, City workers and myself, the only librarian.

I am fascinated by the idea of leadership in the Western countries and our obsession with it, but was also disappointed that none of the facilitators could tell me anything about ethnic-minority leadership. This is Canada, a multicultural country, where in 2002 there were 3 million visible minorities who represented 13 per cent of the non-aboriginal population aged 15 years and older (Statistics Canada, 2003). In 2006, 5,068,100 individuals called themselves visible minorities (Statistics Canada, 2010).

What is ethnic-minority leadership?

Ethnic-minority leadership is different from cross-cultural leadership. Cross-cultural leadership issues generally focus on a leader from the Anglo-Saxon culture learning about the nuances of the cultures they have to do business with to be successful and profitable. It focuses on this leader's ability to incorporate the kaleidoscopic nature of the cultural variables into their everyday business activities. Ethnic-minority leadership is about identifying potential candidates from minority groups within Anglo-Saxon cultures to become leaders in whatever field they are in and providing them with the support and training necessary. This could mean upgrading their education, technical, language or leadership skills, or simply encouraging them to live up to their fullest potential at work and recognizing them for their contributions.

Who are visible minorities?

The Employment Equity Act (1995) defines visible minorities as "persons, other than Aboriginal peoples, who are non-Caucasian in race or non-white in colour" (s.3). The Commission for Racial Equality, a public body from the UK that deals with racial discrimination and which has merged to become the new Equality Human Rights Commission, states that "visibility is a vague term that could refer to a number of things including phenotype [observable characteristics] accent, dress and name" (Office for National Statistics, 2007). These statistics include visible minorities of all generations.

So, why focus on these new immigrant visible minorities?

Note that the terms ethnic minorities, visible minorities, new immigrants, immigrants, are all being used interchangeably and they all mean minorities living in majority white countries.

In 2005, the Toronto City Summit Alliance, a coalition of civic leaders that focuses on many initiatives in the City including DiverseCity in Toronto in Canada, reported, "Immigrants already provide 60 per cent of our population growth. By 2020, they will supply 100 per cent" (Siddiqui, 2005). Statistics Canada (2005) adds that "roughly one out of every five people in Canada, or between 19 per cent and 23 per cent of the nation's population, could be a member of a visible minority by 2017 when Canada celebrates its 150th anniversary ... Canada would have between 6.3 million and 8.5 million visible minorities 12 years from now." Canada is not the only country experiencing immigration growth with a focus on visible minorities. Australia, another multicultural country similar to Canada, also reports a growth in its immigrant population. Immigration has also been a significant factor in contributing to Australia's population growth but has been more volatile. In 1993, immigration contributed about 23.1 per cent to population growth and in 2008, this rose to 59.5 per cent (Australian Government, 2009). According to the Australian Bureau of Statistics (ABS), the immigrant landscape has changed in Australia as well. It is not just immigrants from English speaking countries that arrive to live in Australia; in 2007, of the 647,000 immigrants "the majority (76 per cent) were born in other than main English speaking countries." People born in the UK contributed to the largest group of overseas-born Australian residents, closely followed by China, India and Italy, in that order, in large numbers.

In the United Kingdom, in 2001, 4.9 million (8.3 per cent) of the total UK population was born overseas and an estimated 223,000 more people migrated to the UK in 2004 (Office for National Statistics, 2005). BBC news reported that "people born in Asian or African countries accounted for 40 per cent and 32 per cent respectively of all applications, the principal nationalities being Pakistani, Indian and Somalian" (BBC News, 2006). In the United States, where multiculturalism is not a clearly established policy at the federal level, "slightly more than half (53 per cent) of resident non-immigrants were citizens of Asian countries" (Baker, 2010). The United States also has a healthy Latino and African-American population who are visible minorities. People have always migrated to the United States, Canada, Australia and the United Kingdom, but recently the social make-up of immigrants coming to these countries has changed. It is no longer Europeans moving between countries, but the non-Caucasians from different countries that come from different age groups, with different levels of education,

Table I.1	Regions of birth, proportion of Australia's population – selected years at 30 June

	1999	2004	2005	2006	2007	2008	2009(a)
	%	%	%	%	%	%	%
Australia	76.9	76.2	75.8	75.4	74.9	74.2	73.5
Oceania and Antarctica (excl. Aust.)	2.4	2.7	2.7	2.8	2.8	2.9	3.0
North-West Europe	7.9	7.4	7.3	7.3	7.3	7.3	7.2
Southern and Eastern Europe	4.6	4.3	4.2	4.1	4.0	3.9	3.8
North Africa and the Middle East	1.2	1.3	1.4	1.4	1.4	1.5	1.5
South-East Asia	2.8	3.0	3.0	3.1	3.2	3.3	3.4
North-East Asia	1.6	2.0	2.1	2.3	2.4	2.6	2.8
Southern and Central Asia	0.9	1.3	1.4	1.5	1.8	2.1	2.3
Americas	0.9	1.0	1.0	1.0	1.1	1.1	1.1
Sub-Saharan Africa	0.7	1.0	1.0	1.1	1.1	1.2	1.3

(a) Estimates for 2008–2009 are preliminary – see paragraphs 9–10 of the Explanatory Notes.

Source: ABS: http://www.abs.gov.au/ausstats/abs@.nsf/Products/0549A6756B213B 25CA25776E00178A59?opendocument

economic background and status (refugees) that constitute the new immigrant population in all these countries and they are the very visible minorities.

Considering the number of visible minorities that live in these countries, especially here in Canada, it is baffling and perhaps even shameful that there was not much literature on minority leadership. After all, many of these minority immigrants would or could have been leaders in their profession or their community at some point in their lives.

Focus of this book

This book will focus on visible minorities as in those who are non-Caucasian and have certain obvious characteristics that set them apart, such as accent, dress, etc., who work in the field of libraries and information sciences. Although visible minorities of all generations will find this book useful, first generation visible minorities will find it particularly useful and relevant to their work experiences. This is because, even though the second and third generation visible minorities are visible minorities, they do not see themselves in the same way as do first generation minorities who are trying or struggling to fit in. In spite of the differences in physical appearances, if any, second and third generation visible minorities are citizens of the country that their parents or grandparents emigrated to and have assimilated into the culture of the country in which they were born, in terms of education and cultural and professional experience. Because of this, they do not face the same challenges that first generation visible minorities do. One major challenge that first generation visible minorities face is the cultural differences between themselves and their new host country. The book does not focus on Aboriginal populations or smaller populations who have lived within a country for many generations, such as French Canadians in Canada, but touches on challenges faced by African-American populations in spite of having lived in the US, the UK or Canada for generations. Indigenous populations in Australia, the United States and Canada will need whole books dedicated to the challenges they face as minority groups and how this may have an effect on their leadership skills and abilities.

Not long ago, Barack Obama, a visible minority in the United States of America, was contending to be the President of the country. The world was watching because, not only was America having its elections, but also a black man was trying to be the leader of that country for the first time in its history. Although he was of mixed race (white mother and a Kenyan father), and was raised by his mother, Stanley Ann Dunham and her family, he was seen as the black man, a visible minority. He did not have the experience or a glorious resume like his competitors (example: Hilary Clinton), and yet, due to various different factors that played a big role in the election campaign, he won. To the world watching, what was obvious during this election campaign was that it is not easy for a visible minority to assume a leadership role in a country where the majority of the population is white. Readers should know that Obama was born in Honolulu, Hawaii, in the United States. His father was a student in the United States and married his mother Ann, an American citizen, and so Obama is both a first generation immigrant and a visible minority due to his African-American appearance and roots. If he had had a Ukrainian or Serbian father, he would not have qualified as a first generation visible minority. If becoming a leader can be challenging in itself, becoming a leader as a visible minority is even more challenging as seen in Obama's election campaign.

While the political leadership role is about securing votes from different population groups by earning their respect, leadership in libraries is about many things including that, and also education, experience, confidence, being collaborative, being accepted and finding the right opportunities both within and outside of the library field. Leadership is also about the willingness of the individual to become a leader and the willingness of the society (in this case the information field or the organization, such as an academic or public library) in accepting an individual as their leader.

Ethnic minorities who come to Western countries as new immigrants have many hurdles to jump through. The processes they have to go through (paper work, medical check-ups, and police records checks) to get to their new countries are disheartening and tiring. Once they are in their new countries, their educational or professional credentials from their home country are quite often not recognized by their new country. They need to upgrade their education, which they cannot do without money, they cannot have money without a job and they cannot have a job without a proper education. It becomes a vicious cycle, one which they need to find a way out of before they can consider leadership. It is not due to lack of education that they cannot find jobs; it is due to lack of recognition and acceptance of their education: "Visible minority population is generally more educated than the rest of the Canadian population. In 2001, 23.6 per cent of visible minorities held a university degree, compared to 14.2 per cent of non-visible minorities ... despite being more highly educated than non-visible minorities, visible minorities have higher unemployment rates than their counterparts" (Perreault, 2004). It is no wonder that many of these highly educated visible minorities live below the low-income threshold (ibid.). Another daunting concern is the cultural differences they face. They may have a strong accent or have trouble speaking in a way that locals understand. Dr Tien (1998: 34) states that people in the United States find European accents to be prestigious but Asian or Latino accents make their "owners" seem ignorant, uneducated and unequal. Many of these visible minorities can speak grammatically perfect English, but perhaps not the way local folks understand them.

On my very first day in Canada I was taken to Dairy Queen (a fast-food joint) for lunch. The person who took me there ordered for me and left me to wait in line for my food. The woman at the counter asked me a question and all I could understand was that it had something to do with "Sunday." I assumed she was asking if I wanted to get my food on

Sunday (this being Thursday) and replied that I wanted it today. She was puzzled and pointed to the ice cream beside her. I had no idea that there was an ice cream called "sundae." Accent and lack of knowledge of local food were my barriers, not lack of language. After 16 years of living here, I have acquired and mastered this accent to the extent that colleagues are surprised when I mention I had most of my education in India. They assume I moved here at a very young age.

So, because of these simple yet surmountable hurdles that many immigrants face in their new lives, immigrants have more challenges and may or may not be interested in a perfect job that nurtures them to be leaders. Their focus might just be on survival and nurturing their future generation. Unless there is help, they may not think of leadership as an option for them at all. If they don't, then the leadership of countries such as Australia will not be an appropriate representation of their demographics.

Diversity in diversity

Individuals within these diverse cultures are not alike. They differ in their personalities, because of where they are from and what they believe in, in their financial and legal status in their new and home country, in their education, religious beliefs and age. There are differences in psychological and emotional attributes that vary from one human being to another regardless of their backgrounds and current living conditions. It is important for all involved (minority groups and Anglo-Saxons) to remember that not all minority groups or individuals within a group are the same. There are many differences between the different people who come from various countries in Africa, and the same applies for the population that comes from one country in India.

Minority leadership

Once ethnic minorities manage to cross over the above-mentioned hurdles, and manage to accomplish goals and make their way towards leadership, there are still challenges to face. There are stereotypes about minority leaders: they can only lead minority followers; they lack confidence or skills that white leaders have; they are ignorant of their new culture and only do things the way they did in their own culture. The following chapters in this book will attempt to dispel such stereotyping and myths about minority leaders and their ability to adapt to their new majority culture, and will attempt to highlight the kind of cultural strengths they bring with them. The following chapters will also help minority leaders overcome their fears and find ways to become leaders in their fields, particularly in the library and information fields.

Literature on minority leadership in libraries

In library literature, most of the articles about ethnic or visible minorities focus on the subject of collections or programing for multicultural populations, but not much on building leadership skills in ethnic minorities. American librarians have written about librarians of color and their struggle to find jobs or become leaders. Riggs (1999) mentions the lack of leadership literature in libraries prior to 1981. Since then, many articles and books have emerged on library leadership, but as Weiner (2003: 14) observed, "it is clear that many aspects [of leadership] have not been addressed and that a comprehensive body of cohesive, evidence-based research is needed." By "aspects" Weiner refers to the different characteristics, styles and skills that make a leader; I would like to include ethnic-minority leadership as an aspect. Or, it can be considered one "facet" of library leadership that has not had enough attention from leadership writers. When speaking of diversity issues in the same article, Weiner only mentions male and female leaders, not ethnic leadership.

Some efforts to focus on this aspect of leadership are already under way or well established: for example, the American Library Association (ALA) and Association of College and Research Libraries (ACRL) and their efforts to improve retention, recruitment and advancement of librarians of color. ALA established the Spectrum Scholarship Program in 1997; a program that focuses on recruiting under-represented ethnic-minority librarians into the profession. The Association of Research Libraries (ARL) launched its Leadership and Career Development Program (LCDP) in 1997. This 18-month program prepares under-represented librarians from different ethnic groups for leadership roles in ARL libraries. Since ARL has Canadian and US research-extensive institutions as its members, this program is also available for Canadian librarians who are interested. I have not had any luck finding similar programs in Australia or the UK.

I can hear readers asking, "Why should there be a different program or book for ethnic-minority librarians? Why don't they take the same programs as other Americans, Canadians or Australians?" There are three major reasons: 1) many of the leadership programs are tailored for the majority culture, for participants who are familiar with the rights and wrongs and dos and don'ts of their own culture; 2) libraries themselves have European/American value. Although many cultures have had and continue to have libraries, libraries of the Western culture have their own values. They play an integral role in informing, educating and entertaining the haves and have-nots of their societies with a number of free services and programs. Ethnic minorities in their new homes should understand both the culture of their new land and the value of libraries there; (3) the concept of "leadership" varies in different countries. While there are some commonalities of this concept of leadership among various countries, there are differences as well. Many countries would define a leader as honest and trustworthy, and other countries expect their leaders to have experience and therefore be wise. Some cultures see a leader as being authoritative, having the final say in matters, and other cultures see a leader as part of a decision-making group. A single facet of leadership does not appeal to all cultures uniformly.

Some of the first generation immigrants will land in library professions and will need a handbook of leadership etiquette. First generation immigrants are used to different orientations, contexts, and sense of time, and many, many, many cultural differences that add to the already confusing concept of leadership. Both immigrants and their Anglo-Saxon cohorts need to understand the cultural differences that affect leadership styles and skills in order to be well-rounded, efficient leaders in ethnic-minority leadership situations, and I hope that this book will be the first stepping stone towards such an understanding.

Chapter 1, entitled Leadership as defined by culture, profession and gender, clarifies that a definition of leadership is not possible due to various factors that go into building a leader. There are cultural, socio-economic, political, religious, and various other influences, and these have an influence on a leader's performance and behavior. However, it is important as an ethnic-minority librarian to be aware of these influences and self-evaluate.

Chapter 2 attempts to differentiate between leaders and managers. Although leadership is almost indefinable, there are qualities that make leaders who they are and these qualities are different to what is required from managers. Ideally, all managers should be leaders and all leaders should have managerial abilities. Having said that, there is a distinction between these two qualities, and this chapter outlines them. One important thing to remember is that leadership is not about a title. Anyone within an organization can be a leader: take initiative, offer creative solutions, foresee problems, be visionaries, establish goals for self-improvement, encourage and enable other employees. Being visionaries and foreseeing problems come with experience.

Chapter 3 focuses on leadership styles. Leaders come with many styles: authoritative, democratic, pace-setting, coaching, coercive, etc. Each style has a time and a place. There were and continue to be many theories on leadership and some of these theories established certain styles as requirements for leaders. In the early days, the Great Man theory indicated that leaders were born. They came from aristocratic or rich families, were educated and well respected in the community. Trait theory, behavioral theory, contingency theory and situational theory have their own take on leadership styles. Trait theory expected leaders to have certain characteristics and implied that one just had to have distinguishing traits to be a leader. Behavioral theory suggested that leaders were defined by their behavior. Task-oriented or task-focused behavior and good people skills were great qualities, but these alone did not make one a good leader. Many task-oriented employees in an organization are keen on accomplishing tasks, but have no leadership skills or interests. Leadership goes beyond accomplishing tasks. Situational and contingency theory focused on the situation that would cause or mold a leader. A situation defines a leader and the effectiveness of a leader is contingent on how well a leader's style works for the organization.

These theories and styles will continue to evolve as libraries move more and more towards virtual environments, where body language is absent. In such a scenario, one has to refine communicating styles, conceptual skills, and time-management skills to work with various time zones and timelines for different projects and have exceptional people skills to reach their virtual partners. Motivational skills – the ability to be self-motivated and the ability to motivate others – are required skills in a leader.

Chapter 4 focuses on some of the indispensable skills for anyone in a leadership position. Multitasking abilities are expected from all employees and as a leader one has to multitask efficiently without losing focus, as there are many tasks and deadlines. Leaders need to have effective time-management skills and be extremely organized. In Western culture, time-management is an important skill. One of the first things foreign students learn in universities during their orientation sessions is the importance of "time" in Western culture. Assignments have to be submitted on time, classes start on time and even public events and social occasions start and end on time. For immigrants coming from many parts of Asia, Africa and the Middle East, these rigid "time" rules are unusual, especially in public and social settings. The polychronic attitude towards time needs to be left behind to succeed in any career in the Anglo-Saxon culture. Critical thinking skills, conceptual skills, decision-making skills, communication skills, fiscal skills, and people skills are all important skills to learn and use. The communication of information differs between cultures. Some cultures see effective communication as essential and value the social aspects of communication, and others see its value only in terms of information.

Chapter 5 looks at library leadership in three major library types: academic, school and public libraries. While there are many articles on the leadership trends and issues in academic libraries, there is not much literature on the leadership issues and trends in public and school libraries. This disparity could be due to various factors. One such factor is that academic librarians are expected to publish. Public and school librarians generally are not expected to publish. School libraries have a limited number of journals dedicated to their issues. But recent literature on all three libraries suggests that there is an interest in leadership issues. While there are some articles in the academic field that focus on minority leadership in their libraries, it would prove challenging to find such material on public and school libraries. Chapter 5 also provides details on the survey conducted among ethnic-minority librarians, deans and directors of libraries, and directors of library schools in the UK, the US, Canada, and Australia.

Conclusions

For some, leadership comes naturally. For many others, leadership is confusing. There are traits, skills, styles, and behaviors, and all of these are influenced by the individual's cultural, socio-economic, religious, and educational backgrounds. There are values that good leaders have or are expected to have. With minority immigrants there are two layers of culture – the culture they are from and the culture to which they have to adapt – to tackle, and this is not always an easy task. There could also be language issues. Leadership is a learning experience and it takes time, effort, and lots of patience by all involved for an ethnic minority to become a successful leader and to stay in that position.

References

American Library Association. *Spectrum Scholarship Program*. Web. October 13, 2010.

Australian Bureau of Statistics. *3412.0 – Migration, Australia, 2008–09. Regions of Birth*. Web. August 2010.

Australian Bureau of Statistics. *6250.0 – Labour Force Status and Other Characteristics of Recent Migrants, Australia, November 2007*. Web. September 12, 2010.

Australian Bureau of Statistics. *3412.0 – Migration, 2008–09*. Web. April 12, 2011.

Australian Government. Department of Immigration and Citizenship. *Population Flows: Immigration Aspects, 2007–08 Edition*. 2009. Web. September 21, 2010.

Baker, C. Bryan. *Estimates of the Resident Nonimmigrant Population in the United States. Population Estimates, 2008*. DHS Office of Immigration Statistics. Web. September 25, 2010.

BBC News. *Thousands in UK Citizenship Queue*. 2006. Web. September 23, 2010.

Canadian Department of Justice. *Employment Equity Act*. Ottawa. 1995. Web. September 15, 2010.

Locker, Kitty and Isobel Findley. *Business Communication Now*. Canada: McGraw Hill Ryerson. 2009. Print.

Office for National Statistics. United Kingdom Government. *News Release: Reversal of North to South Population Flow Since the Start of the New Century*. London. 2005. Web. September 20, 2010.

Office for National Statistics. United Kingdom Government. 2011 Census. *Ethnic Group, National Identity, Religion and Language Consultation: Summary Report on Responses to the 2011 Census Stakeholders Consultation 2006/07*. London. 2007. Web. September 2010.

Perreault, Samuel. *Visible Minorities and Victimization.* Canadian Centre for Justice Statistics Profile Series. 2004. Web. September 15, 2010.

Riggs, Donald E. "Academic Library Leadership: Observations and Questions." *College & Research Libraries* 60.1 (1999): 6–8.

Siddiqui, Haroon. "Why Hugging an Immigrant is a Good Idea." *Issues Facing Our City Region.* Toronto City Summit Alliance 2005. Web. September 23, 2010.

Statistics Canada. Minister of Industry. *Ethnic Diversity Survey: Portrait of a Multicultural Society.* Ottawa. 2003. Web. September 15, 2010.

Statistics Canada. *Study: Canada's Visible Minority Population in 2017.* 2005. Web. September 25, 2010.

Statistics Canada. *Canada's Ethnocultural Mosaic, 2006 Census: National Picture.* Ottawa. 2010. Web. October 6, 2010.

Tien, Chang-Lin. "Challenges and Opportunities for Leaders of Color". *The Multicultural Campus: Strategies for Transforming Higher Education.* Eds. Leonard A. Valverde and Louis A. Castnell. CA: Altamira Press. 1998.

Weiner, Sharon G . "Leadership of Academic Libraries: A Literature Review." *Education Libraries* 26.2 (2003): 5–18. Print.

1

Leadership as defined by culture, profession and gender

Abstract: There are many variables that go into the making of a leader. Culture, which in itself has many variables (race, religion, language, etc.), is one such variable. To understand ethnic-minority leadership one has to invest in understanding cultural influence, in developing cultural intelligence, social intelligence, and to having an open mind on the part of both the ethnic-minority citizens and their Anglo-Saxon cohorts. It is important for both to understand each other's cultures, to bring their strengths and experiences and work together towards leadership. Due to the different variables, leadership can be confusing or even stressful for those already on its path. Leadership is not for the faint-hearted. Women, considered as minorities in societies, have had their struggles to attain leadership positions.

Key words: leadership and culture, gender in leadership, cultural intelligence, social intelligence, emotional intelligence, leadership in war, leadership in sports, leadership in business, managers and leaders, discrimination

Leadership and culture

Leadership is an enigmatic and complex concept on which a plethora of material has been written, often without ever defining the term. Why is it so difficult to define leadership? Every culture, every occupational field, every individual within these fields and cultures has their own perceptions of leadership. This is because leadership and leaders are influenced by their culture, their personal characteristics, their experiences, situations in life, societal, economic, religious, and political factors, and much more. For ethnic-minority immigrants living in Anglo-Saxon majority cultures, their native culture plays a significant role in shaping them as leaders. Focusing on cultural differences is not meant to stereotype ethnic minorities living in Western cultures, but just to emphasize the role of cultural influences in a person. Culture defines human psychology and therefore one's behavior.

What is culture?

Like leadership, culture too has various definitions. Definitions of culture depend on who is offering them – humanists, anthropologists or sociologists. It is generally accepted that culture defines thoughts, ideas, behavior, and the structure of people living in a society. Culture is about the ways in which people are used to living within their geographical boundaries. Culture is influenced by climate, natural surroundings, and people who occupy the area. Culture is logical, contradictory, complex, with shared assumptions, priorities, and practices. Kluckhohn (1965) defined culture as consisting of patterned ways of thinking, feeling, and reacting to various situations and actions. Marsella et al. (1979: 57) go further to say that, "culture and the individual are mutually constitutive. The individual perceives, interprets, and acts as he does (partly) because of his culture, and in perceiving, interpreting, and acting in that way he (and others) makes his culture what it is."

Given these interpretations, it is evident that an individual and his/her culture are inseparable. An individual's thoughts, behavior, and language is shaped by culture. Though human evolution did not begin with the origins of culture, "culture itself must be congruent with the features of human physiology and psychology that are vestiges of earlier evolution" (McCrae, 2009: 207). Humans are cultural animals and their personal characteristics mesh with the society and customs that condition their behavior. Gandhi's non-violence strategy was an influence from his early introduction to Jainism – an ancient Indian religion that prohibits violence even towards the smallest creatures on earth. Martin Luther King and Nelson Mandela were influenced by the segregation that was all around them. All three also had Western world influences because of where they lived or where they went for higher education. Gandhi was educated in England and had visited South Africa where Nelson Mandela also lived. Martin Luther King lived in the United States. The last two were also influenced by Gandhi's non-violence movement. In all three cases, their own culture (Indian, black or African-American) was a major influence on them: they became leaders to change things around them, to educate people, and to achieve freedom.

A study justifying culture for behavioral patterns, especially with relation to minorities living in white cultures, is probably avoided or questioned due to fears that it might verge on stereotyping. Much of the earlier leadership literature was written by researchers from Anglo-Saxon cultures about minority cultures, and was perhaps biased. This fear has been around for a long time and Scherer and Brosch (2009) have addressed this in their article. They state that:

> Systematic differences in personality and emotionality in members of different races and nation states can be traced back to the earliest human writings, such as those by Greek historians ... In the last few decades,

this approach has been widely shunned and designated as speculation and stereotyping ... [But] like many classic ideas, however, it is often seen to have a kernel of truth and is thus difficult to eradicate completely.

(Ibid.: 265–266)

Accepting cultural influences is not about confirmation bias or ethnocentricism, but is about acknowledging the definitive possibility of the influence of native culture in immigrants.

How does culture shape a person?

There are many ways in which culture shapes a person: religion, economy, politics, language, all contribute towards this. The idea of individualism in cultures plays a major role in shaping one's personality. Asian cultures emphasize "we," as in society as a whole, while American culture emphasizes the importance of an individual, as in "I." In Asia and Africa, the emphasis is on fitting into the society and therefore being interdependent. American and European cultures emphasize independence. As Gardener et al. (1999: 321) noted:

> One clear distinction that emerges between members of Western and Eastern cultures is the extent to which the self is defined in relation to others. This distinction has been referred to as egocentric versus sociocentric selves, individualism versus collectivism, and independence versus interdependence, and focuses on the extent to which the self is defined as an autonomous and unique individual or is seen as inextricably and fundamentally embedded within a larger social network.

Probably because of their emphasis on "I" rather than "we," American and European cultures are at the opposite end of the pole to Asian and African cultures when it comes to behavior in individuals. While Americans and Europeans are, generally speaking, more extroverted, Asians and Africans tend to be more introverted, especially so if they are minorities living in Western cultures. Asians and Africans living in Western cultures are, again generally speaking, usually happy to be followers, while Americans and Europeans have historically aimed to be conquerors and therefore leaders. Asians and Africans have had their share of conquering, but that was well in the past. Non-Caucasian cultures are happy to adapt, while Americans and Europeans are more prone to reject or question decisions before considering accepting. Some of these characteristics could also be due to political influences within cultures. In totalitarian states, followers worship their leaders (they are either forced to or trained to); in a truly democratic culture, leaders and their decisions are questioned. In a democratic country where the majority of the population is poor, working class or uneducated, leaders are often left unchallenged and unquestioned by their followers. There is no implication that Asian and African cultures are lackadaisical, but just that their approaches to issues are different due to cultural and personal differences, and this could be misinterpreted by host countries. In recent times, this idea of thinking as a group has changed. Probably due to Western influences or influences within cultures, and the introduction of popular social media such as You Tube and Facebook, cultural values are changing. For example, Locker and Findlay (2009: 109–110) state that:

> Japan's traditional culture emphasized the group, but there is evidence that this cultural value is changing in new historical conditions. According to research and

analysis by David Matsumoto, Japanese cultural norms such as the sacrifice of one's personal time for the company, avoidance of disagreements with one's boss, and the favouring of compliance over individual initiative have become part of Japan's business past. Modern business values in Japan place more emphasis on the individual person's goals and accomplishments.

Asian and African cultures also emphasize respect of elders. It is not just bowing to or saluting their elders, but following orders from their elders without questioning them. When people from these cultures move to the United States or Canada and are placed in positions where they are to take responsibility and make decisions, they are not completely comfortable. They are not totally sure if they really have complete freedom or if they should run everything by their superiors. In some cases they misunderstand independence and completely ignore updating their superiors. Workplace culture in their host country may also contribute to their leadership behavior when it comes to decision-making and independence at work. If their first job experience in their host country was under an authoritative leader, they are not going to learn the idea of independence at work as it exists in the North American culture. Countries like India, China, and Malaysia in Asia (to name just a few), and many African countries, have authoritative leadership style. Employees are told what needs to be done and how. They are given deadlines to complete projects. They don't get a pat on the back or freedom in choosing how they accomplish their work. The hierarchy of the organization and the employee's role in the organization are made clear. Leaders have titles and authority and most certainly maintain a power distance. Only recently has this begun to change; in many IT-based industries in India young workers are given a voice and asked to participate instead of follow: "Infosys Technologies in Bangalore, India, started a Voice of Youth program, which gives top-performing young employees a seat on its management council" (Griffin et al., 2010: 307).

Like everything else, leadership is a learning experience. It takes time for minorities to adapt to their new culture (both of their host country and their organization) and they would feel less marginalized if they were to find encouragement and mentorship from their white cohorts. With proper training, a good workplace environment, understanding superiors and co-workers, and time on their side, minority librarians will gain an understanding of their new culture, and gain the confidence to learn to make decisions. If the cultural natives have three challenges – organizational culture, adaptation of individual style to fit the organizational culture, and the culture of their land (native) – to deal with, minority librarians have four challenges. They can bring their strengths from their native culture but they also have to learn the ways of their new culture.

Figure 1.1   Four layers of challenges for minority librarians

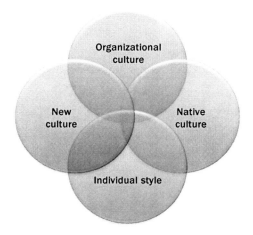

Many immigrants also come from competitive environments within their home countries. This competitiveness causes a conflict in the collective culture. In spite of the cultural philosophy of working and thinking collectively as a whole, in China and India, probably due to their very large populations, students in school, college, and university have to perform competitively to get better grades and win scholarships to better schools either at home or in Western countries. They learn to be competitive at a young age. Being competitive in these cultures means not sharing your means and resources – focusing on the self to get ahead. They are bent on their own achievements and accomplishments, which also causes a lack of trust of others. They do not talk about how much work they have done, which sources they used to complete their assignments, which Western universities they have applied to, or how they might have got their visas to other countries so quickly. They do not want another person competing too closely with them. If they bring this attitude with them to their host countries and continue to foster it at work, it can cause many misunderstandings among their colleagues. The lack of trust that comes from competitiveness can be another cultural issue to deal with. Since libraries are collaborative workspaces, trust is an important issue that minorities need to deal with.

Refugees who seek asylum in North America, the United Kingdom, Australia or elsewhere may also be experiencing survivor's guilt. Survivor's guilt is a condition that affects the mental state of those who survive a traumatic event and move on to better lives when others could not. They often blame themselves, and this causes emotional damage that can also affect self-confidence. Survivor's guilt feelings are usually paradoxical. These survivors may not feel very motivated to be successful, but also appreciate that they have a better life. Some immigrants also have a fear of success.

They are afraid of the barriers that may cause between themselves and their family members still at home. They welcome financial stability so that they can help these family members, but they are afraid of becoming too different as a result of the influence of their new culture or the successes that it offers. This fear is heightened if the immigrant is a very visible minority. Success in their new country could mean losing one's self-identity. For the first few years of their life in their new culture they work on overcoming these fears and guilt before becoming completely assimilated (if they ever do) into their new societies. Immigrants arriving in other countries have all sorts of anxieties. The process of immigration in itself is very stressful: there is a lot of paperwork to be completed, pictures to be taken, referees to be contacted, money to be spent in Canadian, American or Australian dollars or Euros and Sterling, depending on where they are going. This is money they don't have in plenty due to vast differences in the exchange rates of their local currencies. An American dollar is worth Rs. 44 to Rs. 50 depending on the currency fluctuations, and the average Indian salary is not more than the equivalent of $65 to $70 a month. If the immigrants are arriving as students, they have to sit multiple exams in many cases. To come to North America and the UK, students have to prove their English language skills by scoring a certain number of points in the Test of English as a Foreign Language (TOEFL), or the International English Language Testing System (IELTS). Depending on what they choose to study, they may have to complete a Graduate Record Examination (GRE), a Graduate Management Admission Test (GMAT), a Biomedical Admissions Test (BMAT) or a reasoning test or Scholarly Aptitude Test (SAT). All of these exams cost them in dollars and pounds too. If they gain good enough scores, then they have to undergo health checks, character background checks (with police involved), and attend interviews at their local embassies. Immigrants leave their home countries for various reasons such as wars, religious persecution, to seek a better education, a better lifestyle, to explore new cultures, or to find a new life. Some immigrants suffer from familial separation anxiety, because, in many cases, the whole family is unable to come for various reasons. These are some of the many, many reasons that cause personal and cultural behavioral patterns in an individual.

A comprehensive essay on how cultural differences impact leadership qualities is almost impossible to offer because culture is not easy to define and it is not the only influence that shapes an individual. Where an individual lives, family, economic status within their home culture, educational background, and personality, also contribute to their leadership qualities. As McCrae (2009: 205) states, "human mentality and personality were shaped primarily by culture, which was itself a relatively arbitrary product of history and geography." He goes on to add that "culture [itself] must be congruent with the features of human physiology and psychology..." (ibid.: 207). In today's global world, there is no longer a single factor that dominates a personality. For example, children in India watch children's programs televised from America, Australia and the United Kingdom. They are no longer influenced only by the culture into which they are born, but by all that they watch in their formative years. Does this mean that future generations of Indians will have a different mindset from the generation that exists today? Only time will tell.

Minority librarians and majority white cohorts need to be aware of their cultural differences when dealing with each other. This may clarify behavioral patterns and allow one to ask questions to clarify a situation rather than assume. Intercultural or cross-cultural work experience can create a vibrant, knowledge-rich, creative work environment, but only if seen in a positive light by both parties.

It should also be mentioned that acculturation happens to these ethnic minorities but the pace at which it does may vary depending on at what age they arrive in a new country, how strong their beliefs were (political, religious, and cultural), etc. Being aware of cultural differences, acknowledging their impact on the individual, and adapting to behavioral change when needed are the first steps towards leadership.

How can leaders learn to be aware of cultural differences?

What is cultural intelligence?

Since culture plays such a vital role in shaping a person, it is important that ethnic minorities pay attention to who they are, what they are doing, what the culture around them is doing, and how they are different. This will enable a person to learn the differences and how to work effectively with the differences. Visible minorities living in a majority white culture need to learn to be culturally intelligent to work efficiently and effectively. Being culturally intelligent refers to "a person's capability to adapt effectively to new cultural contexts" (Earley and Ang, 2003: 59), and not necessarily to complete assimilation. Cultural change is a good challenge to adapt to and accept since the ability to adapt to change is a vital requirement for leadership roles. On that same note, it is also advisable that the majority culture realizes these cultural differences and reciprocates cultural intelligence. They should understand the different cultural personalities that surround them.

Apart from learning and adapting, cultural intelligence is also about mutual trust. If, as a leader, an individual who is an ethnic minority has problems with trust in a collaborative environment, it is advisable to do a self-check on what is causing this. There could be many reasons for this mistrust (such as negative job experiences from the past), but in the case of a minority librarian it is worth looking into the cultural issues as well. In third-world or developing countries, many of which were occupied and ruled by the European colonizers and where everyday living could be a challenge, people learn not to trust each other. This same strain of mistrust can also be seen in the natives towards their majority occupants. With minorities living in majority Anglo-Saxon cultures, different ethnic-minority groups develop mistrust towards each other. A poll conducted in the US in 2007 reports, "61 per cent of Hispanics, 54 per cent of Asians and 47 per cent of black respondents would rather do business with whites than members of the other two groups" (Hastings, 2008). This may not be a widespread mentality in the library field, but both the minorities and majorities in this field would do well to be aware of this. Learning about the behaviors of different cultures, and the reasons behind them, then being able to adapt, is cultural intelligence.

Librarians coming from various minority cultures are also influenced by the politics of their countries: a black immigrant from South Africa (during apartheid) might say that he/she has never been allowed to take control of a situation let alone make decisions. Then there are cultures where men are dominant and women are not allowed or expected to make decisions. A female librarian from this cultural background is possibly surprised and hesitant when placed in a position to make decisions. Minority librarians need to overcome these cultural hurdles in order to become culturally competent librarians and then leaders. If in any doubt, it is advisable to seek constant feedback from all diverse perspectives involved in order to identify and overcome problems. Cultural awareness and self-awareness are two important steps towards becoming a minority leader. If an individual is one of the very first or one of very few minority librarians hired by an organization, it is also important to realize that one may be a role model for any future minority librarians hired.

Self awareness can happen through self-evaluations and workplace evaluations. Self-evaluation is left to the individual's willingness to learn to acknowledge weaknesses and learn to change. With workplace evaluations, an individual's strengths and weaknesses as a functioning employee can be identified. In the United States and Canada, newly-hired workers in all fields are evaluated constantly. Depending on the field or the organization, workers can be evaluated anywhere between every three months, every six months, once a year or every two to five years. In many public libraries in North America, librarians need to pass a probation period of six months, after which they will be evaluated every year. In academic libraries where librarians are hired as faculty, they go through renewal processes and tenure tracks which expect them to show that they are competent and are progressing in their position. Most of these evaluations are carried out by their supervisors or managers. There is always the danger of these evaluations being too subjective. Quite often these evaluations are not explicit in identifying a person's potential, but they are a step in the learning process of the self. In North America, there is also the humbling 360 degree evaluation where all colleagues who work with you – be they your subordinates, peers, supervisors and managers – evaluate you under various categories. This is also known as the multi-rater or multi-source feedback. All of these evaluations should be seen as stepping stones towards success – learning experiences to better one's self. This kind of monitoring/evaluating is essential for leadership behavior. Self-monitoring cannot be done without social intelligence skills.

What is social intelligence?

Social intelligence refers to "the ability to understand the feelings, thoughts, and behaviors of persons, including oneself, in interpersonal situations and to act appropriately upon that understanding" (Marlowe, 1986: 52). Very similar to cultural intelligence, social intelligence is about social awareness. Having social intelligence promotes flexibility in one's behavior, by providing a better understanding of society, of feelings, thoughts, and behaviors in individuals, and shapes one's decisions and responses accordingly. This is another important step towards leadership: understanding an individual's behavior.

What is emotional intelligence?

Emotional intelligence (EI) is the ability to listen and empathize, the ability to recognize and regulate emotions in oneself and others, and the ability to communicate effectively. Kreitz (2009) observes five domains of EI: self-awareness, self-regulation, motivation, empathy, and social skills. With these EI skills, leaders should be able to take a proactive approach to issues that might be brewing within the organization or an employee. The ability to create a workplace culture that encourages interaction among people and develops shared service values among co-workers creates good leaders. When service values are shared, employees feel responsible for their contribution to their workplace and this in turn motivates them to be more involved with their assignments. With emotional intelligence, leaders can lead with influence and understanding and achieve goals.

Just as the idea of leadership differs between cultures, it also differs in every occupational field.

Leadership and occupation

Leadership in every field is also defined by the nature of the occupation, not without commonalities. In the field of nursing, ward leadership aims to improve the care experience: "A ward leader needs to be well equipped, educated and motivated to perform in that role" (Waters, 2010).

In war, leadership is about accomplishing missions. *Leadership in the Canadian Forces: Doctrine* defines leadership in the Canadian forces as: "directing, motivating and enabling others to accomplish the mission professionally and ethically, while developing or improving capabilities that contribute to mission success" (Canadian Forces Leadership Institute, 2005: 5).

In sports, leadership is about success. It can be achieved independently or in a team environment, as in playing as a team with one common goal: achieving success.

In business, leadership is about making profits, which ultimately is about success. But today's businesses focus not only on profits, but triple-bottom line reporting: the economic, social and environmental success of a business.

In all fields, leadership is about good behavior, being self-aware, enabling others, showing accountability, developing thinking skills to make better decisions, working as a team, progressing, accomplishing, and being successful.

Libraries, like most organizations, are dynamic and complex entities. In libraries, leadership is no different from any other industry. Leadership in libraries is about caring for users and their experiences as users, caring for staff and their needs, finding and implementing innovative ideas, working on projects and accomplishing success, and, for a truly business experience, working with vendors to negotiate prices for products so a decent budget can be maintained. Librarians work collaboratively to achieve success, much like a sports team does. It is about achieving success in providing and matching the right source to the right user. Today's librarians are no longer just keepers of books, but, by providing and meeting the informational needs of their users, they create scholars and educate and entertain their users, which in turn helps create an intelligent, self-reliant, truly democratic society. As librarians, they motivate, mobilize, and enable others, which are all leadership qualities. Unfortunately, many librarians don't recognize this quality in themselves. Often, others within the organization, or outside of it, don't recognize this quality in librarians either. Librarians provide information and mobilize and enable their society and have a role in its successes.

A library's organizational culture changes due to the many variables that affect social interactions at work, much like any other organization. It is important for a leader to understand and remember the fact that a library as an organization is a growing and evolving organism. The library leader needs to understand how his/her library functions, what changes may occur, how to deal with them proactively, how to come up with creative solutions and be aware of the role of their library within the parent organization. A leader should not only be capable of dealing with the different situations and problems that come their way, but should go beyond what is expected of them and come up with creative ideas and innovative solutions.

Can leadership be taught?

The fact that most of the literature available on leadership tries to explain leadership qualities or describe the skills required by leaders rather than define leadership itself tells us that leadership is not an exact science. Leadership is about styles and skills: leaders need to have certain skills to succeed and learn different styles of leadership so that they know which one to use, and when. Skills and styles can be taught in a classroom. In *Leadership Can Be Taught*, Parks (2005) has a whole chapter on the first day of classes at Harvard University. Professor Ronald Heifetz teaches a class on leadership using case-in-point methodology and his first day of class is nothing more than conversations and questions that go back and forth between him and his students. In this method of teaching, "what goes on in the classroom itself is an occasion for learning and practicing leadership within a social group ... The class also has a clear and challenging purpose – to make progress in understanding and practicing leadership" (ibid.: 7).

It is evident that leadership can be taught and learnt in a classroom. It can also be learnt informally – from experience, education, self-awareness, and self-evaluation. As a minority librarian, experiences will abound and it is important to learn from these experiences. Becoming a leader (with a title attached to your name) takes time and practice. Developing trust, showing accountability, and proactive behaviors are all steps towards leadership. Minority librarians should not focus on acquiring titles or climbing each rung of the professional leader for success. Commanding respect with actions and decisions, regardless of the title or position one holds, can lead towards leadership. Alire (2001) calls this marginal leadership. Marginal leadership is about influencing in non-traditional ways, without fancy titles such as Director, Dean or Head of a Department. There are many leaders, even among non-minorities, who influence and command from the margins. From this perspective, many leaders in a library may not even be librarians. But because of who they are and how they deal with issues, they command respect. To do this, one needs to be self-critical and evaluate:

- What are my strengths and weaknesses?
- What are my limits? What can I do and what can't I do?
- What will I do and what will I not do?
- What have I done wrong in the past and what did I learn from it?

Managers as leaders

Libraries have managers. Although some managers can be leaders by the nature of their jobs (they have a title, they mobilize their team members, and motivate them to achieve goals), most are just managers in the sense that they manage, control their employees to be productive, and meet their library's goals. These managerial managers look up to higher-level management for directions towards the future of their organization. A leader-manager on the other hand has a vision, influences others, provides direction, makes tough decisions, and creates and directs change as necessary to lead the organization through its best, and its tough, times.

Leadership and discrimination

Leadership is not for the weak and faint-hearted. It is for those who are able, competent, and trustworthy and can command respect through their actions and behavior. It is for those who can face their weaknesses and have a willingness to learn from them. A leader should possess certain basic qualities such as humility, simplicity, diligence and determination, and follow ethical practices in order to be effective in a multicultural environment. A leader cannot afford to be too sensitive to comments and minority librarian leaders need to remember this. It is true that, in some cultures, being a minority of a certain ethnic group and living day-to-day life might in itself be a challenge. But as leaders, librarians need to rise above this. As Alire (2001: 102) put it, "It is not easy being a minority, in almost every aspect of daily life except within one's family. It makes one develop the tough skin that is necessary for many leaders of color to lead. Better said, emerging leaders should not take adversity and conflict personally." It is important to focus on the job that needs to be done rather than worry about discouraging or disparaging comments from co-workers. However, if a problem of acceptance persists within an organization regardless of all the efforts by a minority employee, then the problem could lie within the organization and needs to be addressed. Talking to the individual causing the issue may clear up a lot of the problems. It is possible that the person causing the issue isn't even aware of how disruptive they are. Talking to a trustworthy co-worker is advisable. This way, others know that a problem exists. Another self-reliant tool is to keep a record of all the issues that arise, so that there is some evidence to present to higher authorities if the situation gets out of hand. If all these strategies fail, then there are laws in the country. In Canada, the Canadian Charter of Rights and Freedoms is a binding legal document that protects the basic human rights of all Canadians. The Racial Discrimination Act in Australia (1975) aims to protect Australians of all backgrounds and ensure that they have the same opportunities. Other statutes and charters to know about are: the United Nation's International Convention on the Elimination of All Forms of Racial Discrimination (ratified in 1965 and entered into force in 1969); New Zealand's Race Relations Act (1971); the Human Rights Act (1993); the Human Rights Amendment Act (2003); South Africa's Constitution of the Republic of South Africa (1996); the Promotion of Equality and Prevention of Unfair Discrimination Act (2000); the United States' Equal Pay Act (1963); the Civil Rights Act (1964); the UK's Race Relations Act (1976); the Human Rights Act (1998); Ireland's Employment Equity Act (1998); the European Union's Convention for the Protection of Human Rights and Fundamental Freedoms (1950); and the Treaty of Amsterdam (1999).

Every country, and possibly different jurisdictions within countries, has their own laws on human rights.

Women and leadership

Women dominate the library field numerically and hence there are many female managers and some leaders. But the focus here would be on female ethnic-minority librarians. There are no known statistics on the number of female ethnic-minority librarians working in Canadian libraries. The Canadian Library Association (CLA) informed the author that it does not collect information on the ethnicity of librarians for understandable reasons. This means that, unless a survey is sent out to all the librarians in Canada (in all provinces and territories, and covering school, public, regional, special, college, and university libraries) and assuming participants would be willing to provide this information, it would be impossible to assess how many female leaders come from ethnic minorities.

But as an ethnic minority, to become a leader one has to follow the same principles of leadership that are recommended to their Anglo-Saxon cohorts. Being aware of oneself and others will help on the way to leadership. Since leadership can be taught and learnt, ethnic minorities can learn and develop a style that fits their personality and work culture. Seek mentors who understand cross-cultural management. Some ethnic-minority women come from a culture where men are dominant and make decisions around the home and may not share domestic work responsibilities. Regardless of their education, experience, and background, these women may have to take a secondary role or may play no role in decision-making at home. Even though many of the minorities who come from abroad are well educated and Westernized in their external appearance (in their clothes, hairstyles, and make-up), they may follow their cultural traditional roles at home, and many women may accept these without complaining.

In Western cultures, it is only recently that women have started to break the glass ceiling and attain leadership roles. If this is the case, one can imagine the challenges an ethnic-minority woman from a background such as that described above would have to face as a leader. Turock (2001: 114) quotes Margaret McIntosh's four phases of leadership where women are concerned: Phase I is Womanless Leadership; Phase II is Women as a Leadership Anomaly; Phase III is Women as Leaders; and Phase IV is Leadership Redefined. It is in the final phase that female leaders are inclusive. Modern leadership theories that include the contributions of women have filled a hole in leadership theories. This Phase IV is the reconstruction of leadership by including all kinds of leadership patterns crucial for future success. Although as a feminist McIntosh is talking about gender balancing in leadership roles, equity of leadership, as in the inclusion of ethnic minorities for leadership roles, can also be added to this phase. As Turock says (ibid.: 129–130):

> To date, while issues in leadership have been approached on the basis of gender, little has been done to discern the issues vis-à-vis ethnic and other non-majority-women leadership. While some women have made progress in leadership ranks, it is predicted that it may

take an additional 75 to 200 years to overcome the inequities of African American women in gaining and retaining leadership positions.

Hopefully, it will not take that long for other ethnic-minority librarians to gain and retain leadership positions. According to the World's Women 2010 Report by the United Nations (2010), women worldwide have a long way to go in terms of high-level leadership positions. Women are highly under-represented in decision-making positions at government levels and in the private sector, with only "13 of the 500 largest corporations in the world" having a female CEO. This in spite of the fact that women are predominant in the fields of education, health and welfare, social sciences, and humanities and arts.

There are well-known popular leaders such as Oprah and there are lesser-known successful leaders such as Banaree Bennie Wiley (CEO of The Partnership) from minority cultures. But, as Turock implies, there aren't enough of them to strike a balance either within the library field or elsewhere. Bennie was one of the very few African-American women who graduated from Harvard Business School in 1972. She became the CEO and President of The Partnership, Inc., in 1991, where she had been working for over 20 years. What Bennie was most appreciative of during her path to leadership was "the value of inclusion and social networks for ethnic minorities' career success and quality of life" (Roberts, 2007: 343). Unless minorities feel included and appreciated for their differences and trained to be leaders, there will not be a balance of leadership.

So what is leadership?

So, can we arrive at a definition of leadership after reading this chapter? Leaders are influenced by the culture they are from, the culture they live in, their personality (which again is a result of their culture), and the demands made on them. Leadership is about mobilizing people, predicting future directions, leading your team towards success, caring about people who work with you and who depend on your services. But this alone does not define a leader. Leadership is also about styles and skills, and about using the right styles and skills in the right place at the right time. Each leader has his or her own style, which may or may not work in different situations. For an ethnic-minority leader living in North America, the United Kingdom, Australia, etc., it is important to know and use the right style in the right situation. How does one know the right skills and styles for the right situation? Self-awareness, cultural awareness, and social intelligence will all help in learning and building skills and styles.

References

Alire, Camila A. "Diversity and Leadership: The Color of Leadership." *Journal of Library Administration* 32. 3/4 (2001): 95–109. Print.

Canadian Forces Leadership Institute. *Leadership in the Canadian Forces: Doctrine*. Canada: Chief of the Defense Staff by the Canadian Defense Academy. 2005. Print.

Earley, P. Christopher and Soon Ang. *Cultural Intelligence: Individual Interactions Across Cultures*. Stanford: Stanford University Press. 2003. Print.

Gardner, Wendi. L., Shira Gabriel and Angela Y. Lee. "'I' Value Freedom, but 'We' Value Relationships: Self-construal Priming Mirrors Cultural Differences in Judgement." *Psychological Science* 10.4 (1999): 321–326. Print.

Griffin, Ricky W., Ronald J. Ebert, Frederick A. Starke and Melanie D. Lang. *Business.* Toronto: Pearson Canada. 2010. Print.

Hastings, Rebecca R. "Poll Finds Mistrust Among Racial Groups." *Human Resource Magazine.* BNET, February 1. 2008. Web. May 5, 2011.

Kluckhohn, Clyde. *Culture and Behaviour.* New York: The Free Press. 1965. Print.

Kreitz, Patricia. "Leadership and Emotional Intelligence: A study of University Library Directors and Their Senior Management Teams." *College and Research Libraries* 70.6 (2009): 531–554.

Locker, Kitty O. and Isobel M. Findlay. *Business Communication Now.* Whitby, Ontario: McGraw-Hill Ryerson Ltd. 2009. Print.

Markus, Hazel Rose and Shinobu Kitayama. "Culture and the Self: Implications for Cognition, Emotion and Motivation." *Psychological Review* 98.2 (1991): 224–253. Print.

Marlowe Jr., Herbert. "Social Intelligence: Evidence for Multidimensionality and Construct Independence." *Journal of Educational Psychology* 78.1 (1986): 52–58. Print.

Marquis, Bessie L. and Carol J. Huston. *Leadership Roles and Management Functions in Nursing: Theory and Application,* 6th ed. Philadelphia: Wolters Kluwer Health/ Lippincott Williams and Wilkins. 2009. Print.

Marsella, J. Anthony, Roland G. Tharp and Thomas J. Ciborowski. Eds. *Perspectives on Cross-Cultural Psychology.* San Francisco: Academic Press. 1979. Print.

McCrae, Robert. "Personality Profiles of Cultures: Patterns of Ethos." *European Journal of Personality* 23 (2009): 205–227.

Parks, Sharon Daloz. *Leadership Can Be Taught: A Bold Approach for a Complex World.* Boston: Harvard Business School Press. 2005. Print.

Roberts, Laura Morgan. "Bringing Your Whole Self to Work: Lessons in Authentic Engagement From Women Leaders." *Women and Leadership: The State of Play and Strategies for Change.* Ed. Barbara Kellerman and Deborah L. Rhode. San Francisco: Jossey-Bass. 2007. 343. Print.

Rothstein-Fisch, Carrie. *Readings for Bridging Cultures: Teacher Education Module.* Boston: Harvard Business School. 2003. Print.

Scherer, Klaus R. and Tobias Brosch. "Culture-specific Appraisal Biases Contribute to Emotion Dispositions." *European Journal of Personality* 23 (2009): 265–288.

Turock, Betty J. "Leadership in the Library and Information Science Professions: Theory and Practice." *Women and Leadership.* Ed. Barbara Kellerman and Deborah L. Rhode. New York: The Haworth Information Press. 2001. 111–132. Print.

United Nations. "The World's Women 2010: Trends and Statistics." *The World's Women Reports.* New York: Statistics Division Home. 2010. Web. April 15, 2011.

Waters, Adele. "Leadership Challenge: One Trust's Policy of Giving Ward Leaders Supernumerary Status Has Given Them the Confidence to Effect Change." *Nursing Standard* 24.51 (2010): 242.

2

Managers and leaders

Abstract: Management and leadership are two different concepts. They are sometimes used interchangeably. Not all managers are leaders and not all leaders have management skills. Managers are not expected to be visionaries whereas leaders generally are. Managers forecast future implications based on evidence, whereas leaders have a vision and will lead their organization towards it. Some people are natural leaders and others need a lot of encouragement and motivation. Motivation is a key factor in preparing future leaders and a skill that is common to both managers and leaders. Without motivation, there can be no leaders or managers.

Key words: leaders and managers, origins of managers, origins of management, evolution of management, managers and leaders, library leaders, library managers, motivation, teamwork, motivation theories

Who are leaders?

On the first day of a leadership workshop offered through the University of Saskatchewan, the instructor wrote on the board "leadership is ..." and asked participants to fill in the rest. Each of the 27 participants had their own interpretation of leadership. There are no agreed-upon definitions of leadership or leaders. The concept of leadership differs based on many things, and it can be domestic, global, gender based, and culture based. Every culture has its own idea of and ideals for leaders. In Latin America, leadership is masculine, authoritative, and aggressive. In the US, leadership focuses on the bottom-line, and in Japan, leadership is for the wise and elderly. In other words, it is for those with many years of experience, not for those who climb the organizational ladder quickly. While an educational degree such as an MBA is important for leadership in countries such as the US and Germany, it is not so vital in many countries of Africa. Age does not factor in the US, the UK, Germany, France, and Poland when leadership is considered, but it is very important in Japan, Vietnam, and China. In Asia, it is generally believed that the older one is, the wiser they are. In Germany, the Netherlands, the US and Israel, it is not important for a leader to be from an elite background, but it matters in Latin America, France, the UK, Poland, Japan, China, Africa, and Vietnam (Derr et al., 2002: 289–293). Leadership is personal but should also work for the organization. Within the domestic confines of a country, leadership is further defined by the organization. And within the organization it is further defined by individual styles and traits. The American idea of leadership does not hold true in other countries. Leadership, from available definitions in American literature of the 20th century, can be summed up as rational, management oriented, male, technocratic, quantitative, cost-driven, hierarchical, short term, pragmatic, and materialist.

Alder (1999: 240) cites the Anglo-Saxon origins of the verb to lead as *laedere*, which translates to "people on a journey," and the Latin origin of the verb *agere*, which means "set into motion." In the contemporary world, a leader is seen as a visionary who creates change and helps the organization and its people go on this journey of change. It is about influencing others to agree on a societal or organizational change. Leaders should make decisions and accept responsibility even when the decision does not reap intended benefits. Leaders should follow the ethical and moral codes of society and the organization. It is agreed that leaders exhibit certain skills and traits. These skills seem to change based on the leader, his/her background, and the situation in which the leader works. Leadership research indicates "that certain personal traits and characteristics are especially important for leaders and for the exercise of leadership" (Mason and Wetherbee, 2004: 188) but the exact nature of those skills remains unspecified. There are over 200 different traits and skills identified by different authors on their research on leadership.

Who are managers?

Management on the other hand has agreed-upon definitions. One such definition is: "it is the process of planning, organizing, leading and controlling an enterprise's financial, physical, human and information resources to achieve the organizational goals of supplying various products and services" (Griffin et al., 2010: 189). Since management is specific to organizations, various books offer variations of this definition. But it is generally agreed upon that managers help in planning, organizing, leading, and controlling. Unless they themselves have leadership skills, managers cannot lead without the help of a leader.

The origin of managers or management

J. B. Say, a French economist, coined the word entrepreneur. He defined the entrepreneur as a person "who directs resources from less productive to more productive investments and who thereby creates wealth" (Drucker and Maciariello: 13). This is not far from any definition of today's manager. One cannot be productive and create wealth without controlling, organizing, motivating, and leading by doing. Say's followers, François Fourier and Comte de Saint-Simon, "discovered" management in the early 19th century, before it actually came into existence. They could see the emergence of organizations and a need for a person to manage them. Prior to this, the idea of an organization did not exist. It was believed that the economy, not humans, was the driving force that dealt with the behavior of commodities. Humans were only expected to adapt. Hence, no concept of organizations and no management. With a systematic blueprint for economic development came the systematic development of management – an area that would focus on managerial tasks – and the tasks of finding ways to improve productivity and relationships among workers and between workers and their superiors. According to Drucker and Maciariello, the management boom happened after the First World War. It was the events that occurred during this war and the handling of it that conceived the idea that "management" could restore the economy. But, with so much destruction all around and the economy down on its knees, there wasn't much will to restore the economy and the first boom of management died here. After the Second World War, sometime during the twentieth century with the economy slowly recovering, Western and European societies "became a society of organizations" by creating various tasks towards restoring the economy and dividing the responsibilities. Whether big or small, these organizations needed management. Management was developed, studied, and practiced as a discipline. Formal and informal organizational structures, business objectives, strategic planning, decision-making processes, business communication models, and marketing processes were all developed and studied during this time. Now, in the era of the global economy and virtual organizations, the study of management still continues to evolve today.

The evolvement of management

After the Second World War, the management of businesses moved from the idea of "ownership" to organizations. As the economy moved to an industrialized and organizational format, management came to be motivated by the needs of the organization and its people. This meant finding ways to increase productivity and profit and dealing with laborers. Before organizations were formed, there were no management positions, just "charge hands" enforcing discipline over fellow peasants (ibid.: 18). With the emergence of management and organizations, production increased and this led to the stabilization of the economy. With a stable economy emerged a developed world. A lack of management and a lack of organizations which divided work into groups and completed them successfully would have meant chaos for the continents that had just come out of two wars. It was management that created the "social and economic fabric of the world's developed countries. It has created a global economy and set new rules for countries that would participate in that economy as equals" (ibid.). While the first world was developing rapidly, countries in Asia were still trying to achieve independence from their oppressors and from there on took many decades to stabilize their own economy, and some of them are still trying to do so. Countries such as India were not open to foreign markets until the mid-1990s, and the idea of organizations and management as it was well established in the West did not exist there until very recently. Management in countries like India was considered oppressive, demanding, and something to obey and perform. So, as these countries develop, their managers, like those in the West a century or so ago, are learning to deal with educated workers. They can learn from the models established by Western or European countries.

In North America, the UK, the US, Australia, and other countries that are open to immigrants, management is undergoing another change. Just as in leadership, the focus of management in various organizations in these countries is now shifting to managing people of different cultures – people that are fundamentally different in their thinking, behavior, languages, customs, traditions, clothing styles, and economic, educational, and religious backgrounds. More challenges are brought about by the fact that these multicultural populations are sometimes not even full-time employees of the organization. They could be contract workers or outsourced employees working a world away from their leaders and managers. In the virtual, multicultural world of work, the functions of managers and leaders continue to be challenged.

These same challenges are being faced by libraries in these countries as well. There are many more library staff and librarians from multicultural populations working in these countries in the 21st century than there were in the previous century, and this is evident from the number of articles and books that are written and published on this topic. There is little material on leadership from minority librarians, but there is some on the hiring and retention of minority librarians in academic libraries.

Are there differences between managers and leaders?

Apart from different definitions, traditionally speaking, there are many differences between managers and leaders.

Management is a position, a function. Leadership does not always have to be a position or title. It is possible that to be considered a leader of an organization (in title, such as a Dean or a Director of a library) one has to climb up the rungs of management. But having a leadership title alone does not make one a good leader. In a library setting, leaders can be anyone from the circulation supervisor, librarians, managers, Dean of the library, to library staff.

Management is generally a mid- or upper-level position in an organization's hierarchy. While leaders themselves are at higher-level positions, leadership itself can come from any position within an organization. A page at a library may have a better vision on how and where to shelve items so that they are better accessible and visible. A manager might be a better judge of how this redesigning of the shelving process should take place. This page is not a leader with a title, but in a small way contributes to the success of his/her organization. This is what a leader does, perhaps on a bigger scale for the whole organization. In the article "The Crisis and Opportunities in Library Leadership," Riggs (2001: 6) differentiates leaders and managers thus:

> Library managers tend to work within defined bounds of known quantities, using well-established techniques to accomplish predetermined ends; the manager tends to stress means and neglect ends. On the other hand, the library leader's task is to hold, before all persons connected with the library, some vision of what its mission is and how it can be reached effectively. Like managers, there are leaders throughout the library. The head librarian is not the only leader in a library. This fact must be remembered and addressed during leadership development programs.

Managers find and work with evidence – the finance, human resources, productivity, and profit and loss of an organization are taken into account when a manager makes a decision. Leaders are expected to think outside the box and make decisions that may challenge this evidence. Leaders might have to make radical changes and decisions whereas a manager might just follow instructions from a higher rung of the hierarchy. There are always exceptions and occasions in organizations where a manager might make radical changes, but this is not the norm.

Management is desk-bound. Although this idea could be challenged in the virtual environment, management focuses on drawing out plans and executing them, which is still desk-bound work. Leaders do not focus on desk work. They focus on reaching out – reaching out to other organizations, to people in the organization, and to other external environments that would maintain the stability of their own organization.

Management is about specifics and productivity. Leadership is about the betterment of the organization as a whole on various levels both at present and in the future, without worrying about specifics. Leaders leave specifics to managers.

Management is administrative. Leadership goes beyond administration. It is about walking the territory, building a network, and knowing powerful people to get the job done.

Management is about recording information. It is up to managers to do job evaluations, maintain expenses, etc. Leadership is about seeking and forming new relationships. Or, as Kouzes and Posner (2007) put it, "leadership *is* relationship." It is a "relationship between those who lead and those who choose to follow" (ibid.: 24). To have followers continue to follow them, leaders initiate new ideas and challenge the old ways.

Management concerns itself with the efficient use of resources. Leadership, while concerned about the efficient use of resources, focuses on finding new sources of resources.

Leadership focuses on the environments outside – those that can affect the organization, those that should be in alignment with the organization, and those that should be avoided and alienated. Managers focus on the internal operations of an organization.

Managers follow protocols and organizational policies. By adhering to rules, they do the right things. Leaders will take the organization to different levels by breaking these protocols and making policy changes. Managers might question or challenge the feasibility of "change" at various levels of the organization, and leaders would like you to believe in the slogan "yes we can" and work towards it. Leaders will need these questioning managers to create and record policy changes and provide a strong structural foundation by having all the written documents in place for the organization.

Managers, by nature of their positions, tend to control. They might be responsible for the finances, production, and human resources of an organization. They cannot do their jobs effectively if they don't find ways to control loss of monies and staff turnover within the organization. Leaders on the other hand like to hear and try out new ideas and encourage others to change and to adapt to change.

Management is more task-focused and leadership is more people-focused. This is not to say that managers don't focus on people and leaders don't focus on tasks. It is important to remember that managers should have human resources skills and leaders need to accomplish tasks.

Managers predict change based on the evidence they have collected. Leaders bring about change.

Managers focus on organizing and staffing. Leaders work on aligning staff to work together towards a common goal.

Leaders establish goals and directions. Managers establish ways to achieve those goals and directions.

Managers are engaged in day-to-day problem solving and leaders are focused on energizing and motivating colleagues, subordinates, and external collaborators.

Managers accomplish and achieve by "driving" their workforce, and leaders do the same through persuasion and influence. But again, whether a leader or manager "drives" or persuades varies, based on the culture of the organization and the style of the leader.

In a library environment, as in many other organizational environments today, leadership and management are no longer solely dependent on one person. One person alone is not expected to have a vision, lead through and implement changes. As Porter-O'Grady puts it, "in today's socio-technical organizations, [organizational] culture is collective ('team'), the expectation is involvement and investment, and the style of implementation is facilitative and integrative. Both staff and management now know that no one person has the only 'best' strategy, vision or methodology for change" (Porter-O'Grady, 1993: 53–54).

In this team environment, managers and leaders are agents of change who depend on the ability and skills of collaborative staff to help provide direction for the organization. For example, the Dean of the academic library may not always have decision-making power but may depend on the collegium's guidance. A Director of a public library may seek advice from the Board. Leaders should see themselves as part of the team or groups of teams within the organization who produce results through joint efforts.

Table 2.1 Managers vs. leaders

Managers	Leaders
Position in the organization	Leadership is a role and can come from anywhere in the organization
Desk oriented, evidence based	People focused and people oriented
Internal focus	External environment focus
Controlling	Motivating and influencing
Implement goals and directions	Establish goals and directions
Administrative	Non-administrative
Supervisor	Coach who may teach, but not supervise closely
Organize	Align
Drive	Persuade

As Clutterbuck and Hirst (2002) mention in their paper, "Leadership Communication: A Status Report," researchers like Warren Bennis, who have tried to distinguish between managers and leaders, have been badly misunderstood. This is not because Warren Bennis's distinguishing factors were inaccurate, but because they struck a strong chord of realism. Some of the distinguishing factors mentioned by Bennis were:

- The manager focuses on systems and structure; the leader focuses on people.

- The manager imitates; the leader innovates.

- The manager accepts the status quo; the leader challenges it.

- The manager's eye is on the bottom-line; the leader's eye is on the horizon.

- The manager does things right; the leader does the right thing.

In today's organizations it is very true that both management and leadership are intertwined. Both managers and leaders manage and lead, and depend on each other's skills to succeed.

Commonalities

Both management and leadership can be taught and learned. Managers can also be leaders and leaders can possess management abilities. From a study conducted by Henry Mintzberg et al. (1998: 4–8) it was concluded that managers do the following:

- Managers work at an unrelenting pace (ibid.: 4).
- Managerial activities are characterized by brevity, variety, and fragmentation (ibid.).
- Managers have a preference for "live" action and emphasize work activities that are current, specific, and well defined (ibid.: 6).
- Managers are attracted to the verbal media (ibid.: 8).

If these are accepted as day-to-day managerial duties, then all of these can be applied to leaders as well. Leaders also work at an unrelenting pace and collaborate with their team. Leaders' activities can be characterized by both brevity and in some cases longevity, and leaders like action.

Managers can be at various levels of the organization: top-level managers, mid-level managers, and first line managers. As previously mentioned, leadership can come from any level of the organization.

Managers are expected to posses certain skills and some of these can also be transferred to leaders: human relations skills, time-management skills, decision-making skills, and conceptual skills (Griffin et al., 2010: 187). Both leadership and management are important for an organization. Leaders create and direct change, while managers create a structure to implement this change in an orderly process. Leaders can keep the organization current, abreast, and aligned with its external environments. Managers maintain stability and coordinate activities at all levels of the organization, internally.

Managers have to "control" due to the nature of the work. There are leaders who control with their authoritative style of leadership. This style of leadership may work for very few organizations – it is certainly not a style for modern-day libraries.

Leaders motivate. Managers also motivate their staff, by allowing them the freedom to experiment and learn by doing. Through motivation, both managers and leaders enable others to act, be productive, and attain a set of organizational goals.

Both leadership and management are art and science. There is a huge body of literature covering both topics where arguments were put forth, analyses made, evidence presented with scientific precision. It is not leadership qualities that are science, but the study of it, and the wealth of literature available on the subject (not necessarily all in the library world) brings it closer to being science. Some would disagree. Mullins and Linehan (2005: 134) state that "the taxonomy of leadership qualities and behaviours cannot be rigorous, as leadership is not a rigorous scientific phenomenon."

Some writers see leadership as an art (Heifetz and Linsky, 2002; Scholes, 1998) because leaders don't always conform to stereotypical behavior but tend to be inventive, creative, and original. Both managers and leaders have to be dynamic, adaptive to changes, and be able to empower others to complete tasks. Empowering others is an art that cannot always be taught in a classroom. Managers and leaders coach others and, again, coaching is both an art and a science.

Some leadership authors call leadership "organic." Schreiber and Shannon (2001: 40) call leadership "a discovery process." Since leaders "need to cultivate a welcoming attitude to leadership problems" (ibid.) by learning from every situation and experience, they see leadership as an evolving organism. As Karp and Murdock (1998: 256) put it, "the quality of leadership is born in an individual's inherent personality and then refined by that individual's life experiences, behavioral choices, attitudinal proclivities, and core values," by which they suggest that leadership is elusive.

Both leaders and mangers are expected to have critical thinking skills, analytical skills, to be efficient coaches, and to be familiar with problem-solving techniques. They should have technical skills, conceptual skills, and human resources skills, although, depending on their position, a combination of some of these skills might be more useful than others. A manager at a lower level might have good technical skills, but a leader at a higher level might be more adept at human resources skills and conceptual skills than technical knowledge.

Both leaders and managers have to work hard to develop trust. As Clutterbuck and Hirst (2002) say, leaders and managers have remarkable resilience. By this, the authors mean that both leaders and managers admit their mistakes when things go wrong, learn their lessons, and incorporate these lessons into their vision. They don't wallow in self-misery.

Both managers and leaders should be aware and self-aware. They must be aware of their actions and the consequences, aware of their mistakes, and be aware of newcomers to the organization, their expectations and experiences. They must be respectful of staff from different cultural backgrounds, be open-minded, be willing to learn, be challenged, and be adaptable.

Both managers and leaders work towards the success of their organizations.

Last but not least, managers do lead people to work towards the organization's goal. And the very best leaders are first and foremost effective managers.

Libraries and their leaders and managers

Library leaders and managers possess the qualities mentioned above. Ethnic-minority librarians who come from various backgrounds should be aware of the differences between management and leadership and how things are perceived differently in their new country in comparison to their home country. It is important to realize one's potential and to have the ability to fit into either management or leadership roles. If being a controlling leader is the style one possesses, this style may not work in today's organizational structures of the Western world which are looking forward to globalization and to working without borders. It certainly will not work for modern-day libraries which continue to be growing organisms, as first identified by S. R. Ranganathan (Leiter, 2003: 417–418), incorporating changes to their structure, their collections, and their relationships with external organizations. If the ability to control, to make decisions based solely on evidence, and to create a schedule for reaching goals are a person's strong skills, then it is important for that person to accept that they may be better suited to a management position. If one is interested in being a leader, then one has to work towards acquiring the skills and traits that are expected of a leader. It is time to let go of the old ways and adapt to the new ways of life in their new home.

Library authorities should be able to recognize potential leaders and managers from various immigrant groups. This should be done regardless of the previous experiences and qualifications these individuals might have acquired in their home countries. A lack of knowledge of local idioms, cultural implications, or accent issues with language should not deter higher-level library authorities from encouraging minorities in trying to become leaders or managers.

Winston (2001) speaks of recruitment theory and of ways of identifying successful leaders in the library profession. He goes on to say that many issues come into play when a person is choosing their profession – not least the role and influence of teachers, counsellors, role models and friends – and the reasons for choosing a profession play a role in later leadership interests within the profession. Winston admits, however, that when it comes to ethnic minorities, it is not clear what career decision process is involved. His research focused on business, science, and engineering librarians in academic libraries (colleges and universities), and children's librarians in public libraries, and the results for academic librarians suggest that "those who did not intend to become academic business librarians, as characterized by the factors that affected their choice of a professional specialty, are somewhat less involved in leadership activities" (ibid.: 27). In many ethnic cultures the push is to follow subjects or fields that will prove lucrative for the student – medicine, engineering, dentistry, etc. If this is true of any of the minority cultures, then many of the ethnic-minority librarians in the UK, the US, Canada, and Australia are accidental librarians who may need motivating to become involved in leadership activities. One also has to remember that some of the ethnic-minority cultures do not have well-established libraries for the library profession to be considered as a career option. McCook and Geist (1993) speak of the library profession as being invisible to potential minority applicants for a number of reasons. For example, a lack of early monetary incentives such as scholarships and tuition waivers; a lack of partnerships with minority groups; and a failure to reach out to minority recruits early enough in their education process. They conclude that "diversity is being deferred by the library profession," and the Association for Library and Information Science Education data proves "that the library

profession has done little in the way of recruiting minorities."
While there are many library associations dedicated to
minority librarians (who are already librarians), the library
profession has a long way to go in proactively seeking and
recruiting minority librarians. McCook and Geist are more
concerned about providing multicultural services when they
speak of a lack of minority librarians; the same concern can
be extended to leadership issues as well. From all the
literature available, there seems to be no strategy in place for
actively attracting or recruiting ethnic-minority librarians to
the profession.

Motivating ethnic minorities

A sense of belonging is the most important factor for
immigrants with regard to their potential for leadership
initiatives. The feeling of "belonging" comes when they feel
secure and settled. At some later point in their career comes
the leadership initiative. As Maslow's Hierarchy of Needs
model indicates, wanting to fit in, and therefore learning
local culture, comes under social needs and is only the third
level of needs. Although Maslow was not referring to
immigrants in particular, his needs model applies to
immigrants as well. Based on his model, immigrants' first
needs are physiological – the need for survival, the need for
food, clothing, and shelter. The second rung on the ladder is
the need for security – the need for a job that provides
present and future security. The third level is social need,
which is the need for companionship.

This is the stage at which immigrants will try to mingle
with society at large and feel the need to learn, or at least
show some interest in learning, local culture. This is when a

Figure 2.1 Maslow's Hierarchy of Needs

Source: Maslow's Hierarchy Chart redesigned by Alan Chapman at businessballs. com – used with permission.

sense of wanting to "belong" arrives. The next level up is esteem needs – a need for status, recognition, and self-respect. Once immigrants find their place in the culture and learn the nuances of their new culture and have a sense of belonging, their esteem needs are satisfied. The final need is the self-actualization need – a need for self-fulfilment. It is at this level of need that one's leadership abilities can be tested. It is at this level that individuals like to develop their capabilities and skills in order to challenge themselves. Of course, what each individual considers challenging will be different. For some, learning to drive in their new country by adhering to traffic rules might be the challenge one looks forward to at this level. Others might look forward to more complex challenges such as leading the organization that they have been working for. But all immigrants, like everyone else, need motivation to seek self-actualization needs.

Leaders and motivation

One of the skills leaders should possess is motivation; they should be both self-motivated and have the ability to motivate others. Leaders have been identified as people who are motivated by the need for power, for domination, for achievement, and for responsibility (Zaccaro et al., 2004: 113–115). Anyone in a leadership position who has no motivation is impotent as a leader and unproductive within the organization. A good leader not only motivates others to do their jobs efficiently but also motivates others to take the lead. Motivation in leadership should not be about career goals, but about enabling and encouraging others to perform towards the success of the organization. This is where leaders can be coaches and nurture leadership skills in others in the organization.

What is motivation and how does one motivate others?

Griffin et al. (2010: 308) define motivation as "the set of forces that cause, focus, and sustain workers' behaviour." Kouzes and Posner (2007) mention two kinds of motivation – intrinsic and extrinsic. They go on to explain these by saying that "people do things either because of external controls – the possibility of a tangible reward if they succeed or punishment if they don't – or because of an internal desire" (ibid.: 115).

Lack of motivation in a person's personal life means not wanting to seek any of the needs indicated by Maslow's Hierarchy of Needs model. Lack of motivation at work means stagnation: stagnation in a position, in productivity, being stuck in a rut. If employees are not motivated, both intrinsically and extrinsically, they are not going to seek out new ways of doing their work effectively. Motivation is not just about "carrot and stick" but about encouraging the heart. Encouraging the heart can maximize an employee's full potential and empower them. It should be followed by both the financial and moral support of the organization. It is not very effective to encourage employees to find new ways of doing a job and then not support them to pursue these new ways. Staff must be given clear direction and the best opportunities possible to do what they do best. This can only be done through ongoing dialogue and by keeping all communication channels open between leaders, managers, and employees. In the library world, new ways of doing a job could mean researching and buying collections in newer formats or introducing new technology for staff – Blu-ray Discs, mobile technology, wireless technology, e-books and journals, digitization, and, more recently, iPads. Motivation is about allowing more democracy, building a supportive work environment, recognizing staff accomplishments, and having less bureaucracy. A democratic work environment is one that offers attainable goals and allows the freedom to challenge. If bureaucracy provides an unattainable goal, or offers too many restrictions, this is as good as not having any motivation at all and in the worst case scenario it could lead to workplace antagonism and defiance.

Team motivation

In libraries, librarians and staff quite often work in collective groups or team environments. Katzenbach and Smith (2005) distinguish groups and teams as two different concepts. They identify a group environment as a place where there is individual accountability, a strong leader, and where the focus is on individual work products. A team on the other hand has individual and mutual accountability, with each individual taking leadership roles, and offering collective work products. An effective team has members whose skills complement each other and who produce a desired result as "one." Katzenbach and Smith (ibid.: 165) define a team as "a small number of people with complementary skills who are committed to a common purpose, a set of performance goals, and approach for which they hold themselves mutually accountable." Ilgen et al. (1993: 247) describe a team as having collective goals or objectives that exist for a task-oriented purpose. Many libraries have departments or project-based groups that function as teams and in such groups there is a leader that participates, engages, and offers directions and suggestions for efficient team performance. It was Parker (1991) who identified the fundamental element of teamwork, the team players and their styles. He identified four distinct styles of team players: the contributor; the collaborator; the communicator; and the challenger. A contributor is task-oriented and dependable for date provision; a collaborator is goal-directed, with a vision, and has the "big-picture" in mind; communicators are process-oriented people persons; and challengers questions the goals, methods, and ethics of the team (ibid.: 63–64). A good team needs members with all these qualities so that there is a balance in the project results. Parker identifies an effective team as one that is informal, comfortable, relaxed, participative, has good listeners, is goal oriented, is open to criticism, and is self-conscious of its own operations (ibid: 21).

Teams are made up of individuals who strive to deliver as one, and this is not an easy task. It takes time for these individuals to work as one. Teams go through four stages in the life of their task-group: orientation, formation, coordination, and formalization. Orientation is when team members get to know each other and the task at hand. Formation is when the conflict begins as teams have suggestions and opinions and try to define the problem. The next phase is coordination, the longest phase where the team focuses on the task. This is also the phase where a team needs focus and direction, and a good leader can offer both. In the last phase of formalization, the group seeks consensus on their accomplished task (Locker and Findley, 2009: 127). This is based on Tuckman and Jensen's five critical stages of successful team building: forming, storming, norming, performing, and adjourning. Forming is the orientation phase. Storming is where ideas are exchanged and conflicts arise. Norming is the stage where team identity is developed and team ground rules and values are laid. Performing is the important stage where the team has gone beyond conflict and has learnt to work efficiently. The final stage, adjourning, is where the team has completed its set task.

Team members should be aware of their strengths and weaknesses. As Parker (1991: 150) says, "develop a plan to optimize your strengths and minimize your shortcomings" and this will help in being an effective team member.

Teamwork has a wholesome effect, where more than one individual's thoughts, ideas, and perspective come into action. This wholesome effect in itself gives credibility to the work produced by a team.

Though some research differentiates between teams and groups, it is often misinterpreted in libraries. The word "team" is used very loosely in a library environment. Such a team could be a committee or subcommittee established to accomplish a task, provide input, offer recommendations, etc., and has someone who acts as a facilitator for the team – to set deadlines, accomplish tasks, and deliver results on time. Such teamwork (in the loosest sense of the term) in libraries should not only focus on immediate supervisors but should involve the top leaders of the organization such as the director or dean of the library. This leader has to motivate teams as they work on various projects and face challenges in the course of their work.

Team motivation is not very different from individual motivation. A team can consist of members from different age groups and different cultures with different understandings and ideas about how to work on the project. A leader needs to identify these differences and work with the idea of "self-interest" of individual members of the team. A leader should also know how to identify and work with the weakest link in the team. The weak link might either need specific directions, or extra motivation, or might need to be retired from the team. Keeping communication lines open among team members and between the team and the leader – with the leader keeping a check on the morale of the team, offering timely, positive feedback, offering constructive criticism where necessary, and developing a sense of accountability in the group – will make teams successful and productive and leave individual members with a sense of achievement and satisfaction.

There are various theories on motivation and two major approaches to motivation in the workplace are discussed here.

Classical theory

The classical theory of motivation states that employees are motivated solely by money (Griffin et al., 2010: 308–309). While this may be true in some cases or to some extent within a job, there comes a time when employees realize they are not functioning at their full capacity to be efficient workers. Many libraries that have trouble hiring due to various factors, such as geography, organizational issues, climatic conditions, use this theory to hire and retain workers. Many librarians will take these positions as their first jobs, but if there are no other motivational factors to retain them, offering the job satisfaction they are looking for, they will move away to greener grass. Whether they will be happy in their new jobs may be questionable, but the institution that originally hired them will be impacted by turnover rates and time and money spent in finding, hiring, and training new librarians.

Early behavioral theory

Early behavioral theory examines the relationship between changes in the physical environment and worker output by using the Hawthorne effect (ibid.: 309–310). Harvard researchers studied the variations in productivity of Hawthorne workers at the Western Electric Company by increasing lighting levels for workers. When lighting was increased, productivity increased. Researchers concluded that workers responded better to the attention they were receiving from management. This has been disputed subsequently. Later research suggested that workers work better when they participate in an experiment and that there are other variables to consider in this experiment. It also said "that output fell when the trials ceased, suggesting that the act of experimentation caused increased productivity" (*The Economist*, 2009). The working environment is very important for all workers in all organizations.

Libraries were traditionally cold places with lots of books and quiet spaces to study. Today's library users and in fact library staff would prefer not to use or work in old-fashioned libraries. They would like a coffee place, a space to socialize, space to work with their laptops and iPads, workrooms to gather in groups and work on a project, study areas, etc. Contemporary library users see a library as a place to gather, collaborate, and socialize. There have been suggestions that while "the future library will need to continue to provide a central, local place for digital objects, the future library will also want to continue to provide a central, local space for reader-users" (Atkinson, 2001: 8). With close to 50 per cent or more of collections available online and many programs available through distance learning (ibid.), in many libraries library administrators are able to provide the much-needed space to users. Leaders in libraries recognized this need and acted on it. Other libraries followed suit. Library staff need updated technology and continued support to be able to use this technology in order to provide access to their collections, to teach patrons and students, to archive information, and to keep themselves abreast of research happening in the library environment. Users demand immediate online help as they are working on a project and librarians are trying to meet this demand by offering help via live chat services and also through phone and email services.

Immigrants coming from a developing or an underdeveloped country who have worked in a library in their own country could find this set up very different from the libraries they are used to. They might come from traditional libraries that are not user-friendly but exist to maintain and protect existing collections. They might be used to a traditional desk, to silencing users on library premises, they may not have used the most current technology, and they may be unaware of inter-library loan procedures as they exist in Western cultures. Not many librarians are completely unaware of newer library models and their services, but this is something to keep in mind when hiring immigrant librarians. They might need more time to learn their immediate environment and the services available to patrons. They "need to be reassured about what they are doing right" (Kumaran and Salt, 2010: 13) and given the opportunities and encouragement to learn.

After the Hawthorne experiment, other related models such as the human resources model, motivation-hygiene theory, and Maslow's Hierarchy of Needs model (discussed previously) came into existence, all related to human needs and the fulfilment of them as a motivation factor. The human resources model states that managers fall into two categories: theory X managers who believe that people are naturally lazy and need to be punished or rewarded; and theory Y managers who believe that people are naturally active, productive, and self-motivated. Theory X managers tend to be more authoritative with an emphasis on control and a focus on the direct supervision of employees, and theory Y managers should be careful not to be taken advantage of by those who might be lazy. A tendency to lean towards being a theory X or theory Y manager (or leader) could be cultural (Griffin et al., 2010: 310). As Den Hartog and Dickson observe, there are cultures where people are believed to be lazy, evil, and who therefore earn distrust. In their words, "distrust prevails in cultures where people are believed to be evil, and as such more monitoring and closer supervision of employees can be expected" (Den Hartog and Dickson, 2004: 262).

Motivation-hygiene theory believes that hygiene factors, which include working conditions, pay, interpersonal relations, and motivational factors such as recognition and the potential for advancement, are all important (Griffin et al., 2010: 311).

Contemporary motivation theories

Two well-known contemporary motivation theories are equity theory and expectancy theory (ibid.: 311–313). The former suggests that people compare their contribution to their job and their position to that of others (who are in a similar position) and expect rewards accordingly. Immigrants move to new countries for a better life, and a better life means earning more money sooner or later. They are not going to find satisfaction in a job that pays the minimum wage or comparatively low wages, at least not for too long, especially if they are educated and are able to pursue some education and upgrade their credentials in their new locality. Many of the immigrants who came to the US for IT-related positions switched jobs frequently simply for more money. The library industry is not as competitive as IT industries once were and probably never will be. But if retention becomes an issue for libraries this is something to be aware of. Of course, not all libraries can afford to pay more – public libraries and some special libraries may be entirely dependent on public taxes or funding and many academic libraries may not get all the grants they were promised. Though promising higher salaries to their librarians may not be an option, it is important for library administrators to review salaries at set intervals to make sure they are offering competitive wages. Another issue in libraries is advancement by seniority. Newly hired librarians and library staff who have very little experience are energetic, enthusiastic, and creative with what they can do within the boundaries of their job. If they are not considered for better positions because of lack of seniority within the organization, there is no motivation factor for these librarians. If these new librarians or staff happen to be desperate immigrants, they might consider doing this job only until they can find a better one.

Expectancy theory says that people are only motivated to work towards rewards they want and that are attainable. If a new librarian has to work for twenty years within a library before getting four weeks' vacation, this is not a huge motivational factor. Regardless of how hard they might work, they are not going to advance much in their career because of institutional regulations such as seniority-based approval and advancement.

Motivation can be accomplished simply by trusting others to do their jobs, by showing appreciation, by recognizing their accomplishments, by reinforcing positive performance behavior, by matching expectations to people's skills, by setting attainable goals, by providing timely, constructive feedback, by providing a clear sense of direction, and by setting standards. Motivation is not about setting low expectations, but about setting expectations that are achievable and attainable, and about providing the right means to reach that goal. Good leadership that can influence with motivation will naturally lead to the success of an organization and the success of its employees, and this in turn will lead to the success of a leader.

There are many commonalities between leaders and managers in all organizations. In libraries, when a manager has leadership qualities and leader-managerial skills they become an asset to their organization. Both managers and leaders should enable their library employees by motivating them to be leaders – to contribute collaboratively and individually to the success of the organization.

References

Alder, Nancy. "Global Leaders: Women of Influence." *Handbook of Gender and Work*. Ed. Gary N. Powel. London: Sage Publications. 1999. 239–262. Print.

Atkinson, Ross. "Contingency and Contradiction: The Place of the Library at the Dawn of the New Millennium." *The Journal of the American Society for Information Science and Technology* 52.1 (2001): 3–11.

Bolman, Lee G. and Terrence E. Deal. *Leading with Soul.* San Francisco: Jossey-Bass. 1995. Print.

Clutterbuck, David and Sheila Hirst. "Leadership Communication: A Status Report." *Journal of Communication Management* 6.4 (2002): 351–354.

Den Hartog, Deanne N. and Markus W. Dickson. "Leadership and Culture." *Nature of Leadership.* Eds. John Antonakis, Anna T Cianciolo and Robert J. Sternberg. London: Sage Publications. 2004. 249–278. Print.

Derr, C. Brooklyn, Sylvie Roussillon and Frank Bournois. Eds. *Cross-Cultural Approaches to Leadership Development.* Westport: Quorum Books. 2002. Print.

Drucker, Peter F. and Joseph A. Maciariello. *Management.* Harper Collins. 2008. Print.

The Economist. "Questioning the Hawthorn Effect." June 4, 2009. Web. October 18, 2010.

Griffin, Ricky W., Ronald J. Ebert, Frederick A. Starke and Melanie D. Lang. *Business.* Toronto: Pearson Canada. 2010. Print.

Heifetz, Ronald A. and Marty Linsky. "A Survival Guide for Leaders." *Harvard Business Review* 80.6 (2002): 65–74.

Ilgen, Daniel R., Debra A. Major, John R. Hollenbeck and Douglas J. Sego. "Team Research in the 1990s in Leadership Theory and Research: Perspectives and Directions." Eds. Martin M. Chemers and Roya Ayman. San Diego: Academic Press, Inc. 1993. 245–266.

Karp, Rashelle S. and Cindy Murdock. "Leadership in Librarianship." *Leadership and Academic Librarians.* Eds. Terence F. Mech and Gerard B. McCabe. Westport: Greenwood Press. 251–264. Print.

Katzenbach, Jon R. and Douglas K. Smith. "The Discipline of Teams." *Harvard Business Review* July–August (2005): 162–171.

Kouzes, James M. and Barry Z. Posner. *The Leadership Challenge*, 4th ed. San Francisco: Jossey-Bass. 2007. Print.

Kumaran, Maha and Lorraine Salt. "Diverse Populations in Saskatchewan: The Challenges of Reaching Them." *Partnership: the Canadian Journal of Library and Information Practice and Research* 5.1 (2010). Web. September 19, 2010.

Leiter, Richard A. "Reflections on Ranganathan's Five Laws." *Law Library Journal* 95.3 (2003): 411–418.

Locker, Kitty O. and Isobel M. Findley. *Business Communication Now*. Canadian edition. McGraw-Hill Ryerson. 2009.

Mason, Florence M. and Louella V. Wetherbee. "Learning to Lead: An Analysis of Current Training Programs for Library Leadership." *Library Trends* 53.1 (2004): 187–217.

McCook, Kathleen de la Pena and Paula Geist. "Diversity Deferred: Where Are The Minority Librarians." *Library Journal* 118.18 (1993): 35.

Mintzberg, Henry, John P. Kotter and Abraham Zale Znik. *Harvard Business Review On Leadership*. Boston: Harvard Business Press. 1998. 4–8. Print.

Mullins, John and Margaret Linehan. "Desired Qualities of Public Library Leaders." *Leadership and Organization Development Journal* 27.2 (2005): 133–143.

Nuvvo. *Transcript of Obama's Speech: Yes We Can*. Web. December 31, 2010: http://barack-obama.nuvvo.com/lesson/4678-transcript-of-obamas-speech-yes-we-can

Parker, Glenn M. *Team Playing and Teamwork: The New Competitive Business Strategy*. San Francisco: Jossey-Bass. 1991. Print.

Porter-O'Grady, Tim. "What Motivation Isn't." *Nursing Management* 13.12 (1982): 27–30. Print.

Porter-O'Grady, Tim. "Of Mythspinners and Mapmakers: 21st Century Managers." *Nursing Management* 24.4 (1993): 52–55.

Powell, Gary N. Ed. *Handbook of Gender and Work.* London: Sage publications. 1999. Print.

"Questioning the Hawthorne Effect. Light Work: Being Watched May Not Affect Behavior, After All." June 4, 2009. Web. January 17, 2011.

Riggs, Donald. "The Crisis and Opportunities in Library Leadership." *Journal of Library Administration* 32.3 (2001): 5–17.

Rost, J. *Leadership from the 21st Century.* New York: Praeger. 1991. Print.

Scholtes, Peter R. *The Leader's Handbook: A Guide to Inspiring your People and Managing the Daily Workflow.* New York: McGraw-Hill. 1998. Print.

Schreiber, Becky and John Shannon. "Developing Library Leaders for the 21st Century." *Journal of Library Administration* 32.3 (2001): 37–60.

Tengblad, Stephen. "Is there a 'New Managerial Work'? A Comparison with Henry Mintzberg's Classic Study 30 Years Later." *Journal of Management Studies* 43 (2006): 7.

Tuckman, Bruce and Mary Ann Jensen. "States of Small-Group Development Revisited." *Group and Organization Studies* 2.4 (1977): 419–427.

Winston, Mark D. "Recruitment Theory: Identification of Those Who Are Likely to Be Successful as Leaders." *Journal of Library Administration* 32.3 (2001): 19–35.

Zaccaro, J. Stephen, Carry Kemp and Paige Bader. "Leader Traits and Attributes." *The Nature of Leadership.* Eds. John Antonakis, Anna Cianciolo and Robert Sternberg. London: Sage Publications. 2004. 101–124. Print.

3

Leadership styles

Abstract: Leadership theories such as trait theory, behavioral theory, and contingency theory are well known. Each of these theories, developed at various times during the 20th century, focuses on various styles for leaders. While the Great Man theory believed in leaders being born as leaders, other theories implied that leaders need to focus on styles and skills that will turn them into true leaders.

Key words: leadership styles, Great Man theory, trait theory, behavioral theory, situational theory, female leadership styles

Speaking in S. R. Ranganathan's style:

- Every leader his or her style.
- Every leader his or her set of skills.
- Every leader his or her organization.
- Every leader his or her strengths and weaknesses.
- Every leader his or her opportunity.

As already mentioned, leadership is about influencing, mobilizing, motivating, inspiring, and enabling everyone to achieve their fullest potential. Persuading and motivating an organization are not easy tasks to accomplish. To do this effectively, leaders are expected to learn and practice, or at least be aware of, different styles and skills that they can use in different situations.

A leader with no leadership style, or with an inflexible leadership style, will not be successful in helping anyone achieve their fullest potential, and as a result will not be successful in leading the organization. Depending on the organizational culture and the expectations from the kind of audience one is leading, a leader may adopt a style that is authoritative, autocratic, participative, democratic, or delegative.

What is leadership style?

Style is the way in which a leader acts. It is the way in which the leader behaves while motivating, influencing, and accomplishing. Style can either be physiological as in body language, voice, eye contact, and words used, or characteristic as in showing humility, or intellective as in being intelligent or an intellectual. Style can be tangible or intangible. The style that a leader uses will depend on the individual's values, beliefs, cultural background, organizational background, and personal preferences. Just as it is difficult to offer one definition for leadership, so too is it difficult to define what styles a good leader should possess.

A leader's style may also be in the eyes of the beholder. A leader may act in a certain way with good intentions, but the interpreter might interpret this behavior entirely differently from how it was intended. Hence the style of a leader is also dependent on the interpretation of the receiver. There are also situational factors to consider in a decision-making process. Depending on the situation, the leader's style may be demanding or just encouraging and motivating. A leader's own behavior, the situation, and the follower's interpretation of both the leader's behavior and the situation all contribute to the style of the leader.

But, if the situation and the follower are removed from the equation, a leader's own style is shaped by his/her own emotions, learning, and experience, and of course the cultural background from which they come. Studies in leadership theories define different leadership styles as necessary and effective in order to be a good leader.

Theories of leadership

The Great Man

In the early 20th century, with leadership literature just emerging, it was believed that leaders were born not made. Many leaders in various fields came from cultured, educated, and rich families, hence that assumption. It was called the Great Man theory. Of course, they were almost all men. As organizations continued to grow and evolve as a result of industrialization and, later, technology, these great men became outnumbered (by the number of organizations that grew up) and outmoded. But this theory is making a comeback according to some leadership researchers. David Cawthone, in his article "Leadership: The Great Man Theory Revisited," shows that this theory has not been completely abandoned. He states that there are innate differences between leaders and followers that make them who they are and proceeds to ask:

> How [then] are we to explain what seems painfully obvious if we refuse to recognize the Great Man Theory as one of many legitimate and meaningful avenues to our understanding of this most elusive topic [of leadership]? In brief, we can't, for unless we are willing to confront those basic philosophical issues that have

challenged minds throughout history, we are doomed to wallow in the obscurity of meaningless observations – observations that describe yet do little to penetrate the mystery of leadership.

(Cawthone, 1996: 4)

Trait theory

With "great man" becoming an endangered species, the next theory evolved. The first few decades of the 20th century focused on trait theory: a theory that argued that leaders needed to have certain traits. Within this argument, trait theory "did not make assumptions about whether leadership traits were inherited or acquired" (Kirkpatrick and Locke, 1991) but implied that all leaders had some common traits. Some of the common traits identified in leaders were: self-confidence; honesty; humility; aggressiveness; intelligence; dominance; energy; height; and knowledge about the job (Griffin et al., 2010: 323). Kirkpatrick and Locke (1991) emphasize that traits matter. While these "traits [only] endow people with the potential for leadership," not all those who possessed these traits could or wanted to be leaders. Since leaders would need more than just these traits to be successful, leadership scholars questioned the effectiveness of this theory. Also, as the list of acceptable traits for leadership continued to grow, and because not all successful leaders seem to possess the listed traits, this approach to leadership was abandoned.

Behavioral theory

Another popular theory was the behavioral theory approach to leadership. This defined leaders not by characteristics but by their behaviors. Leaders or managers were either task-oriented or staff-oriented. Depending on their orientation, their leadership styles varied. Task-oriented leaders focused on achieving their tasks and might adopt an autocratic style. But staff-oriented managers were more worried about the job satisfaction of their employees. Leaders, according to behavioral theorists, were either coercive, authoritative, affiliative, democratic, pace-setting or coaching. As their names indicate, coercive leaders were more controlling and demanding, authoritative leaders led the way, affiliative leaders were empathetic, democratic leaders were participative, pace-setters were forceful in their leading style, and coaches were encouraging and motivating (see Table 3.1 on p. 82).

Situational theory and contingency theory

In the 1960s and 1970s two new kinds of leadership theory emerged. They were the situational theory and contingency theory approaches. While trait theory and behavioral theory focused primarily on the leader him/herself, situational theory focused on the situation (Antonakis et al., 2004: 152). Different situations require different styles of leadership. Different situations also create different kinds of leaders. What would Gandhi have become if India had not been under British rule? Would he have still become the great leader who is fondly known as the Father of the Nation? While situations create leaders, leaders don't always have control of all situations at hand. A successful leader is also one who learns to adapt to different situations. Situational theory focused more on getting the task done than on developing people skills. One might argue that tasks cannot be accomplished without good people skills, but then one has to remember the autocratic leadership style that does get tasks done without focusing on developing human relationship skills.

Table 3.1 The six leadership styles at a glance

	Coercive	Authoritative	Affiliative	Democratic	Pace-setting	Coaching
The leader's modus operandi	Demands immediate compliance	Mobilizes people towards a vision	Creates harmony and builds emotional bonds	Forges consensus through participation	Sets high standards for performance	Develops people for the future
The style in a phrase	"Do what I tell you"	"Come with me"	"People come first"	"What do you think?"	"Do as I do now"	"Try this"
Underlying emotional intelligence competencies	Drive to achieve, initiative, self-control	Self-confidence, empathy, change catalyst	Empathy, building relationships, communication	Collaboration, team leadership, communication	Conscientiousness, drive to achieve, initiative	Developing others, empathy, self-awareness
When the style works best	In a crisis, to kick start a turnaround, or with problem employees	When changes require a new vision, or when a clear direction is needed	To heal rifts in a team or to motivate people during stressful circumstances	To build buy-in or consensus, or to get input from valuable employees	To get quick results from a highly motivated and competent team	To help an employee improve performance or develop long-term strengths
Overall impact on climate	Negative	Most strongly positive	Positive	Positive	Negative	Positive

Source: Reprinted with permission from *Harvard Business Review*. From "Leadership That Gets Results," by Daniel Goleman, *Harvard Business Review 78* (March 2000): 78–90.

Contingency theory states "that a leader's effectiveness is contingent on how well the leader's style matches a specific setting or situation" (Wolinksi, 2010). If leaders were successful in the roles they played, then it was considered a perfect match. Success in this theory was not determined by tasks accomplished, but by measuring the success of a leader's relationships and their effectiveness in accomplishing success for the organization. This theory shifted the focus of the leader from being task-oriented to relationship-oriented (Antonakis et al., 2004: 155). Winston (2001: 519) quotes Dobbs, Gordon, Lee, and Stamps saying "that the aspect of leadership theory that relates most closely to leadership diversity is contingency theory, which is also called pragmatism, realism, and Realpolitik."

Some more recent leadership theories are transformational leadership, transactional leadership, charismatic leadership, and virtual leadership.

While transformational leadership "refers to the set of abilities that allows a leader to recognize the need for change" (Griffin et al., 2010: 325), transactional leadership is about sustaining stability within the organization. Transformational leaders can work with change and some might even thrive in an environment of change, but transactional leaders are not always comfortable with changes in their environment and may not be the best leaders to manage change.

Charismatic leadership depends on the magnetic personality of the leader. While charisma can be an important trait for leaders, not all successful leaders have been charismatic. Winston Churchill was a great leader, but not many would have considered him to be charismatic. On the other hand, John F. Kennedy had charisma. A discussion of whether he was a great leader with strengths and weaknesses, or a charismatic leader, is beyond the scope of this book. The fear with charismatic leaders is that they could have unquestioning followers and this could mean the downfall of an organization, eventually. Having complete faith in any one person and letting them lead as they wish cannot possibly mean success in the long run. And the leader's charisma may not necessarily help with his/her leadership qualities or abilities; it might just be their personality that is charismatic and therefore likeable. Then again, charismatic leaders have their place too: politics and the entertainment industry are great places for charismatic leaders. Being charismatic is an innate quality, not always a learnt one, and this is parallel to, if not similar to, Great Man theory.

Virtual leadership is still a fairly new kind of leadership. As the demographics of organizations change to include outsourcing and contracting various positions to hired workers in other countries, virtual leadership requires a new set of skills. It requires leaders to be able to work with people who are in different states, countries, and continents, in different time zones, from different cultures, and in different work situations. They may not have all the equipment needed, or a power shutdown on a given day might mean that work cannot be processed. Due to a political situation or a religious holiday in their own country, workers might not want to work on a particular day. A virtual leader has to be knowledgable not only about the work of the organization but also about the cultural work ethic of the different groups he/she has to work with, their political scenarios, and any legal issues with various demographics. This leader will depend a lot on email or phone communication where body language remains invisible to the listener. Apart from finding the right kind of leadership style, a virtual leader also needs to have great communication skills.

A leader should be aware of the organization's policies and expectations, its administrative style, its employees and their expectations, its external environment, and its implications on the organization. The leader should be able to adapt his/her style to suit the organizational needs or choose an organization that requires his/her style of leadership. If there is a disconnect between the two styles, it can be disastrous. In January 1997, Elizabeth Martinez resigned from her position as Executive Director of the ALA. As Martin (1996) states, Martinez was "hailed as a strong and visionary leader who would be able to represent the profession effectively while managing this very complex and unruly organization," but Ms. Martinez did not think the ALA was ready to change. There may be other underlying reasons for her resignation, but it came as a shock to the American libraries.

Styles that work

While an autocratic style worked in the industrial era and the post-Second World War era, when the economy was dependent on production from factories, and when managers were the boss and employees followed instructions, it is no longer the style of Western-world organizations, especially in libraries. There will always be managers or leaders in any organization who control, but it is not the norm, and ethnic-minority librarians should be aware of this. In many Asian, African, and Middle Eastern countries, leaders have the final say. In China, for example, historically speaking, leaders have had authoritarian leadership styles. Triandis (1993: 175) confirms this with the observation that a leader is "paternalistic, taking good care of his ingroup." In many Asian and African cultures that are collectivist cultures, leaders are worshipped or feared to the point that they are not questioned. There is an emphasis on hierarchy. Authoritarianism is not the leadership style that is prevalent in the Anglo-Saxon culture of today, but there is no uniformity in style here either. The American leadership style encourages a collaborative effort from all employees in an organization regardless of their positions or titles, but in Australia, as Christina Gibson (1995: 274) states, "Australians indicated less emphasis on interaction facilitation and more emphasis on a directive style, which is more autocratic and benevolent." In her article, in which she compares leadership qualities between four countries, Sweden, Norway, the US and Australia, Gibson believes individualism and masculinity to be more ingrained in Australians than in Americans, and traces this back to the history of ex-convicts having to be self-reliant in order to survive. This historical factor, along with geographical isolation, may have led Australians to prefer goal-oriented and directive leadership practices (ibid.: 273).

Today's work culture is knowledge based, and leaders and managers are managing educated, intelligent, and, in many cases, experienced workers. Autocracy as a leadership style will affect the longevity of employees in an organization's workforce. In the egalitarian work culture of libraries, leadership is a combination of styles and skills. Leaders are expected to be participative, authoritative yet democratic, to be able to balance tasks and people, and to be effective leaders in person and in a virtual environment, to be able to work with vendors, cataloguers, and publishers on a global scale, to work with librarians and staff from different cultures, and to be fiscally responsible. It is an overwhelming task that cannot be done without training and trial and error. As a minority librarian, it is necessary to know that while egalitarianism exists in the work culture, there is also a hierarchy within organizational roles. Not everyone can do everything without approval. Things have to be approved by higher authorities and/or other groups (committees) within organizations, and this culture is very prevalent in libraries.

So, as to which leadership style works is something the leader needs to work at and learn. Transformational leadership style has been hailed as the right kind of leadership style in the West in recent years (Jogulu and Wood, 2008). This is because, as mentioned previously, change is constant in today's work environment, and transformational leaders are considered best suited to leading an organization through changes caused either by internal or external factors. Li (2001) quotes Robert House, Chair of Organizational Studies at the Wharton School of Management, University of Pennsylvania, as saying:

> Organizational leaders in the twenty-first century will face a number of important changes that will impose substantial new role demands. These changes include greater demographic diversity of workforces, a faster pace of environmental and technological change, more frequent geopolitical shifts affecting borders and distribution of power among nation states, and increased international competition.

(Li, 2001: 175)

All of these have an impact on libraries and a transformational leader can enable smooth transformation in times of change. Transformational leaders can bring about this transformation, and Michael Fullan calls this "reculturing" (2001: 44). He goes on to say that leading in reculturing organizations does not mean adopting a chain of innovative ideas implemented one after the other, but "producing the capacity to seek, critically assess, and selectively incorporate new ideas and practises – all the time inside the organization as well as outside of it" (ibid.).

Weiner, too, confirms transformational style as a preferred style for libraries, and goes on to quote Suwannarat's study which reveals that female directors (in libraries) exhibit higher levels of transformational leadership behaviors and therefore are more effective than male directors (Weiner, 2003: 14). But one style alone is never enough for one to be a successful leader. A good leader should be able to combine two or more leadership styles as the situation demands.

Kimberley (2010) discusses six styles of leadership and cites two of those as having a negative impact. Coercive and pace-setting styles of leadership are two styles that decrease employee engagement and therefore have a negative impact. The "Do what I tell you" and "Do as I do now" styles are top-down management styles and don't take into consideration the different work styles of employees. On the other hand, four other leadership styles – authoritative, affiliative, democratic, and coaching – offer employees a chance to understand the organizational goals and therefore engage with them. Kimberley goes on to discuss the importance of the need for multiple leadership styles in today's organizations and the ability of a leader to move seamlessly and naturally from style to style.

Factors in leadership style

There are many factors that contribute to the style of a leader. While cultural background (as in the culture that one knows and grew up in) and organizational culture are huge factors in what kind of leadership style one might develop, age and gender also contribute to leadership styles.

Age has been considered a factor in leadership style. Younger leaders are more energetic, proactive, tech-savvy, likely to experiment and to want to get things done. Experienced leaders are cautious, work more collaboratively, and are more in tune with the emotions of their subordinates.

There is also research that suggests that a leader's age may have an impact upon how active or passive their leadership style is. This does not mean that all young leaders are active and therefore trailblazers, nor that all experienced leaders are passive underachievers. In libraries, younger staff often complain that their senior management is not interested or is too slow in using the latest technology to improve library access, programs, and products. Does this lack of interest in technology have anything to do with the age of senior managers or leaders? Or are younger librarians too eager to use the latest technology available in their jobs?

Considering the fact that many non-European-influenced countries respect their elders as leaders simply by virtue of their age and usually therefore experience, age could be a significant factor in how leaders act and think. A 25-year-old graduate, fresh out of university, may have great leadership skills, may have experience in leading students on campus, but may not have all the experience required to lead a big organization with its various dynamics and politics. While these younger employees are needed and appreciated for their fresh ideas and their readiness to take on challenges and for their technological skills, older employees are also needed and appreciated for their experience, knowledge, and skill sets. Both groups can bring their strengths to the success of the organization. In North America, leadership is not always necessarily restricted to older people. Kakabadse et al. (1998) refer to three leader profiles in their study of the Australian Commonwealth Federal Government – the radicals, the bureaucrats, and the team players – with the first group (radicals) being the youngest, between 25 to 35 years old, the second group (bureaucrats) between 46 to 55 years old, and the last group (team players) being 56 years and over. They noted that older workers were mature and had long-term perspectives, and younger employees were highly energetic, motivated, and competitive.

Table 3.2 Leadership attributes

Radicals		Bureaucrats		Team players	
Positives	*Negatives*	*Positives*	*Negatives*	*Positives*	*Negatives*
Open style	Hypercritical	Committed	Structured	Performance/people oriented	Can appear conservative
Enjoy a challenge	Dislike controls	Respect communication	Intolerant	Communicative	Poor history of change
Committed	Dislike interference	Impartial	Critical of company	Committed	Open to criticism
Encourage dialogue	Need to be in charge	Rules oriented	Negative impact	Encourage checking out	Team driver
Service driven	Dissatisfied	Disciplined	Need to be boss	Mature	Tolerant
Outward focused	Negative view of company	Details driven	Dislike being controlled	Encourage dialogue	Encourage discipline
Follow-through oriented	Naïve	Service conscious	Driven by protocol	Realistic about colleagues/organization	Eclectic approach

Source: From Demographics and Leadership Philosophy: Exploring Gender Differences

In the debate with Vinnicombe (Vinnicombe and Kakabadse, 1999), Kakabadse concludes "that the more mature managers and leaders are, both in attitude and years, the better performer they become." The best-case scenario would be for multigenerational librarians to bring their strengths together and work as one. Many committees in libraries try to recruit a diverse team, a team that is multigenerational, culturally diverse, with varied experiences, and from different demographics. Projects are more successful when people from different backgrounds come together with their own knowledge and skills. The worst-case scenario would be that the experienced leaders do not move forward to try to keep up with the younger generation of users that are using or need to use the libraries, and that the younger employees discount the knowledge and experience that experienced leaders have.

Does gender matter in leadership? Kakabadse in his debate (ibid.) also mentions that "gender is merely a red herring." Many articles and books have been written on whether gender matters, and the answer is no, gender itself does not matter. Women, with their maternal instincts or just plain female instincts, come with their own strengths and weaknesses just as men do. In the 1990s, literature on women and leadership was about the glass ceiling that prevented them from moving into higher positions. But, in Canada at least, that has been changing, slowly but surely. Statistics Canada (2007) reported that more women were employed in 2006 than in 1976. It also reported that 7.1 per cent of women were in management positions in 2006, compared to 6 per cent in 1987, and that 32.5 per cent of women were in professional positions in 2006, compared to 24.1 per cent in 1987.

The Australian Bureau of Statistics (2009) shows that more women have been employed since 1982. Equal Opportunity for Women in the Workplace Agency in Australia reported that as of February 2009, over 30 per cent of women were in

Table 3.3 Distribution of employment, by occupation, 1987, 1996 and 2006

	1987			1996			2006		
	Women (%)	Men (%)	Women as a total employed in occupation (%)	Women (%)	Men (%)	Women as a total employed in occupation (%)	Women (%)	Men (%)	Women as a total employed in occupation (%)
Managerial									
Senior management	0.3	0.8	21.0	0.3	0.7	27.2	0.3	0.8	26.3
Other management	5.7	9.7	30.7	7.8	10.9	37.5	6.7	10.2	36.9
Total management	6.0	10.5	30.1	8.2	11.6	37.0	7.1	11.0	36.3
Professional									
Business and finance	1.9	2.3	38.3	2.8	2.7	46.9	3.3	2.8	51.6
Natural sciences/ engineering/ mathematics	2.3	7.0	19.6	2.3	8.0	19.1	3.2	10.1	22.0
Social sciences/religious	4.3	2.0	61.4	6.0	2.3	68.8	6.7	2.4	71.3
Teaching	3.8	2.6	52.3	5.1	2.8	60.1	5.6	2.8	63.9
Doctors/dentists/other health	0.9	0.9	43.1	1.2	1.1	48.1	1.4	1.0	55.3
Nursing/therapy/other health-related	8.3	0.9	87.1	8.3	1.0	87.0	8.9	1.1	87.4

Artistic/literary/recreational	2.7	2.1	48.4	3.1	2.4	51.5	3.4	2.6	54.1
Total professional	24.1	18.0	50.4	28.8	20.3	54.2	32.5	22.9	55.9
Clerical and administrative	29.7	7.9	73.9	25.6	7.2	74.9	24.1	7.1	75.0
Sales and service	30.0	18.4	55.2	28.6	19.2	55.4	28.6	19.3	56.8
Primary	2.3	7.2	19.7	2.1	6.5	20.9	1.5	5.3	20.5
Trades, transport and construction	2.1	28.9	5.2	2.1	26.4	6.1	2.1	26.3	6.5
Processing, manufacturing and utilities	5.8	9.1	32.4	4.7	8.8	30.6	4.1	8.1	31.1
Total[1]	100.0	100.0	43.0	100.0	100.0	45.4	100.0	100.0	47.1
Total employed (thousands)	5,307.7	7,025.3	–	6,099.0	7,322.4	–	7,757.2	8,727.1	…

[1]Includes occupations that are not classified.

Source: Statistics Canada, Women in Canada: Work Chapter Updates, 89F0133XIE2006000,Table 11, April 2007; http://www.statcan.gc.ca/bsolc/olc-cel/olc-cel?catno=89F0133XIE&lang=eng#formatdisp

managerial positions and 50 per cent of women were professionals (Australian Government, 2009). The United States Department of Labor (2009) also reported favorably on women and their jobs. As of 2009, more women were employed, and it is projected that more women will enter the workforce, to account for a 51.2 per cent increase in the workforce between 2008 and 2018. Women represent over 60 per cent of the workforce in managerial and professional occupations in the United States. But the UK's National Statistics Online (2008) reported that greater numbers of men are employed than women, and that the ratio of men vs. women in the workforce hasn't changed since 1999. The same report also stated that "men are ten times more likely than women to be employed in skilled trades (19 per cent compared with 2 per cent) and are also more likely to be managers and senior officials." Inconsistencies exist in the ratio of men and women employed in different countries, and different provinces or states within these countries. Inconsistencies also prevail in different industries within these countries.

Libraries, as an industry, have traditionally been dominated by women in many of the Anglo-Saxon countries. Libraries in North America, the UK, and Australia are female-dominated organizations. Melvil Dewey, the father of modern librarianship, the man who transformed librarianship from a vocation into a profession by creating a classification standard, by forming the first library school in Columbia and a formal association for librarians, was a pioneer in library education and created career opportunities for women in libraries. He may not have brought women into the library profession for all the right reasons, but, even today, libraries continue to be dominated more by women in these countries (OCLC, 2011). Dewey admitted women into his library school and later hired them as library professionals because they were cheap labor. In 1883, Dewey worked with his friend, Walter S. Biscoe, to reclassify and re-catalog the collections at Columbia College. In order to help Biscoe, Dewey decided to do things that would provide higher gains for lower costs. In his biography of Melvil Dewey, Wiegand (1996: 85) explains, "although he [Biscoe] did not say it, Dewey was, he believed, setting an example for the rest of librarianship; he was recruiting a work force with high character for low cost." Dewey believed that college-educated women had the right "character" for library work and "because they were grateful for new professional opportunities, they would come for less money" (ibid.). Weigand goes on to say that "because by design the institution [library] served and supported the reading canons of a white middle- and upper-class patriarchy, Dewey found it easy to recruit women into the profession in order to fulfill cheaply and efficiently the supporting role he had assigned it" (ibid.: 372). Dewey believed that these women would not be a threat to the dominant culture and that they would be his loyal soldiers.

Australia reports that females dominate the fields of the library and archives professions. As the Australian Bureau of Statistics (2009) states, "Cultural industries where females were noticeably predominant were Libraries and archives (76.2 per cent were females), Arts education (73.8 per cent) and Newspaper and book retailing (64.0 per cent)." The 8 Rs study entitled *The Future of Human Resources in Canadian Libraries* found that females dominated the library profession in Canada as well (8Rs Research Team, 2005). In their report that surveyed libraries and librarians all over Canada, the team found that "overall, females are significantly more represented than males, with nearly eight in ten librarians being female" (ibid.: 43). The team also found significant differences in female representation between managerial and non-managerial positions (see Table 3.4).

Table 3.4   Percentage of visible-minority and Aboriginal librarians by occupational level and by library sector

(Individual Survey; n=1,910)

Library sector	Visible Minority[1]			Aboriginal[2]		
	Total (%)	Non-management/Middle management (%)[3]	Senior administrative (%)	Total (%)	Non-management/Middle management[3] (%)	Senior administrative (%)
Total academic	6	7	2	1	1	2
CARL	7	8	0	2	2	3
Other academic	6	7	3	1	1	0
Total public	7	7	3	1	1	1
CULC	8	8	2	1	1	0
Other public	4	4	4	1	0	1
Total special	8	9	6	1	1	0
Government	6	6	9	1	1	0
Non-profit	11	13	7	0	0	0
For-profit	10	16	0	0	0	0
Total school[4]	6	0	–	0	0	–

Notes: [1]Visible minorities include those who are non-Caucasian in race or non-white in colour (e.g., black, Asian, Middle Eastern, Hispanic).
[2]Aboriginal individuals include those who identify themselves as Status Indian, Non-Status Indian, Métis or Inuit.
[3]Includes non-management, middle management and supervisors.
[4]Results are not presented for senior administrators working in school libraries because of insufficient cases reporting; however, they are included in the total sample results.

Source: 8Rs Canadian Library Human Resource Individual Survey

They also go on to say this about visible minorities in libraries:

> Table 3.4 reveals that visible minorities are not well represented in Canadian libraries, comprising only 7% of the professional librarian labour force (compared to 14% in Canada's entire labour force). The largest portion of visible minorities is found in non-profit and for-profit special libraries (11% and 10%, respectively), although this is still below the national average. Visible minorities are even less likely to be working as senior administrators and this is the case for all but the government sector.

The study also says "little hiring of immigrants is taking place within the library sector."

One reason why women are under-represented in leadership styles could be, as Jogulu and Wood (2008) have found, that women experience disadvantages from prejudicial evaluations. They quote a study by Rutherford (2001), suggesting that women were not accepted as good leaders if they exhibited autocratic, task-oriented, and directive behavior, while this was generally accepted in men. Their paper also discusses women leaders in Malaysia; they mention that this country is slow to advance women in leadership roles due to stereotypical ideas that women are not best suited for these roles. It is librarians and library students coming from these backgrounds who might seek leadership roles in Western countries, and their Western counterparts should be aware of the cultural stereotyping that has tried to keep these women in lower positions. This stereotyping might have caused a lack of confidence and they might not volunteer to lead a team or a committee unless asked.

It is a huge challenge, if not an impossible task, to have visible minorities in leadership roles if they are under-represented in libraries, a challenge that libraries in Canada and other countries should address. And this needs to be done so that visible minorities can play a meaningful role in their societies through all job sectors, not just the government sector. They cannot play a meaningful role in their societies if their jobs just let them live or survive and do not provide them with the challenges they are looking for.

Even though libraries are dominated by women, there aren't too many women in leadership roles. There could be various reasons for this – personal choices that women make, or a lack of experience in the field – or this could be the result of the choices the administration makes for leadership roles.

Do women leaders have a different leadership style?

Much literature has been published on this subject both inside and outside of the library field. Early literature on female leadership styles is not without bias and gender-stereotyping against women. Women are physically and psychologically different from men and, therefore, will behave differently in different situations when compared to men. If women leaders behave like women they are seen as being too soft. Having said that, if a female leader behaves in a masculine way and concentrates on performance rather than working with employees she immediately gets negative attention. On the other hand, again, when male managers are feminine in their leadership style and have a tendency to nurture, they are seen as better, enhanced leaders (Jogulu and

Wood, 2008). When a man demands, the reaction to his leadership style is not so negative and not so swift. On the other hand, a leader who does not manifest masculine perceptions of leadership qualities is not seen as a strong leader either. And some of the challenges faced by female leaders come not from men but from other women who have different perceptions on women leaders. Women leaders have constantly tried to balance their walk between the masculine and feminine styles of leadership in order to be successful. More recent research shows that the differences in leadership styles between men and women are subtle. It is the leadership style of women that is being recommended as the right kind of leadership style by many researchers (Carlie and Eagly, 2007: 133). Carlie and Eagly also point out that the "only consistent difference between female and male managers was that women adopted a more democratic (or participative) style and a less autocratic (or directive) style than men did" (ibid.: 135). But not all women leaders have a democratic style and not all male leaders adopt a directive style. As mentioned previously, today's organizations' leaders do not have all the power to act solo. There are usually various committees and groups, internally within the organization and externally through stakeholders, that might regulate, guide or in some cases control a leader's decision. Like management, leadership, whether it is headed by a man or a woman, is a collaborative effort between various groups of employees within and outside the organization. Library boards, collegiums, and committees play a role big role in a leader's behavior and, therefore, their style.

Minorities who come into leadership roles in libraries, or anywhere for that matter, should be aware of the different factors that have an effect on leadership, and the majority culture needs to keep in mind that cultural background has an effect on the same. Both groups should also be aware that leadership styles have an impact on turnover rates in organizations.

Lack of good leadership can cause the downturn of an organization. Similarly, a leadership style that has no precedence in an organization can also cause internal disturbance. A leader might exude fabulous qualities to his/her higher-ups, but may not be accepted by the subordinate-level employees. If the subordinates do not believe that this leader can or will be ousted, then they may leave for greener grass instead. While this may not be a common occurrence in academic libraries where librarians are tenured, it could still affect the non-librarian staff. Some turnover is a welcome and healthy change for organizations including libraries, but a high turnover rate can cause too much disruption to everyday activities. While librarians tend to stay in their jobs for long periods of time, other staff may not. The 8Rs study concluded that, generally speaking, the Canadian library workforce is for the most part satisfied with their current employment situation (8Rs Research Team, 2005).

In their article entitled "Are Leadership Styles Linked to Turnover Intention: An Examination in Mainland China? Hsu et al. (2003) found that "there was a significant negative relationship between each component … [of leadership style] … and turnover intention." Their focus is on turnover rates in China, but this holds true in other countries and across professions. Sellgren et al. (2007) have found that there is a direct correlation between leadership and turnover rates in nursing. A high turnover rate in the nursing industry has been common for many years in countries like England, Canada, and Sweden, but Sellgren et al. found that a lack of good leadership led to a lack of job satisfaction, which had an effect on the work environment, and this might have an effect on turnover. While nothing could be found in the library literature on turnover rates due to leadership styles, there are plenty of articles on retention issues. Many of these focus on hiring minority librarians in libraries and minority students in library programs.

Maintaining the right level of staffing is essential for the success of an organization. In the library context, too much turnover can cause stress on other librarians who may either have to handle parts of the job that are not being currently covered by any position, or may have to become too involved in the processes of recruiting, hiring, and training. This costs money and time and can also delay in work progress.

Minority librarians need to be aware of all the leadership styles discussed in the leadership literature and find their own style, but they also need to practice moving between styles in different situations. This is where leadership becomes an art. Both minority librarians and their Anglo-Saxon cohorts should be aware of the fact that though leadership has some common attributes, "depending upon the cultural value orientations of a given country or set of countries, the meaning of the leadership situation changes from culture to culture" (Triandis, 1993: 181) and therefore they must be willing to adapt.

References

8Rs Research Team. *The Future of Human Resources in Canadian Libraries*. February 2005. Web. January 25, 2011.

Antonakis, John, Anna T. Cianciolo and Robert J. Sternberg. *The Nature of Leadership*. London: Sage Publications. 2004. Print.

Australian Bureau of Statistics. "6273.0 – Employment in Culture, Australia, 2006: Introduction." March 31, 2009. Web. January 30, 2011.

Australian Government. "Equal Opportunity for Women in the Workplace Agency." February 2009. Web. January 28, 2011.

Carlie, Linda L. and Alice H. Eagly. "Overcoming Resistance to Women Leaders: The Importance of Leadership Style." *Women and Leadership: The State of Play and Strategies for Change*. Ed. Barbara Kellerman and Deborah L. Rhode. San Francisco: Jossey-Bass. 2007. 133–135. Print.

Cawthone, David L. "Leadership: The Great Man Theory Revisited – The Editorial." *Business Horizons* May-June (1996): 1–4.

Fullan, Michael. *Leading in a Culture of Change*. San Francisco: Jossey-Bass. 2001. Print.

Gibson, Christina B. "An Investigation of Gender Differences in Leadership Across Four Countries." *Journal of International Business Studies* 26.2 (1995): 255–279.

Goleman, Daniel. "Leadership that Gets Results." *Harvard Business Review* 78 (March 2000).

Griffin, Ricky W., Ronald J. Ebert, Frederick A. Starke and Melanie D. Lang. *Business*. Toronto: Pearson Canada. 2010. Print.

Hsu, Jovan, Jui-Che Hsu, Shiao Yan Huang, Leslie Leong and Alan M. Li. "Are Leadership Styles Linked to Turnover Intention: An Examination in Mainland China?" *Journal of American Academy of Business* 3.1/2 (2003): 37–43.

Jogulu, Uma D. and Glenice J. Wood. "A Cross-Cultural Study into Peer Evaluations of Women's Leadership Effectiveness." *Leadership and Organization Development Journal* 29.7 (2008): 600–616.

Kakabadse, Andrew, Nada Kakabadse and Andrew Myers. "Demographics and Leadership Philosophy: Exploring Gender Differences." *Journal of Management Development* 17.5 (1998): 351–388.

Kirkpatrick, Shelley A. and Edwin A. Locke. "Leadership: Do Traits Matter?" *Academy of Management Executive* 5.2 (1991): 48–60.

Li, Haipeng. "Leadership: An International Perspective." *Journal of Library Administration* 32.3 (2001): 177–195.

Martin, Susan K. "The Profession and its Leaders: Mutual Responsibilities." *The Journal of Academic Librarianship* 22 (1996): 376–377.

National Statistics Online. "Working Lives." Office for National Statistics. September 26, 2008. Web. January 28, 2011.

OCLC (Online Computer Library Center). "How One Library Pioneer Profoundly Influenced Modern Librarianship." *Dewey Services.* OCLC. 2011. Web. October 24, 2011.

Paterson, Kimberly. "I'm Leading – Why Aren't They Following? Part 1." *Rough Notes* 153.12 (2010): 100, 102–103.

Rutherford, Sarah. "Any Difference? An Analysis of Gender and Divisional Management Styles in a Large Airline." *Gender Work and Organization* 8.3 (2001): 326–345.

Schubert, James N. "Age and Active-Passive Leadership Style." *The American Political Science Review* 82.3 (1988): 763–772. Web. January 30, 2011.

Sellgren, Stina, Goran Ekvall and Goran Tomson. "Nursing Staff Turnover: Does Leadership Matter?" *Leadership in Health Services* 20.3 (2007): 169–183.

Statistics Canada. "Women in Canada: Work Chapter Updates." April 20, 2007. Web. January 28, 2011.

Triandis, Harry C. "The Contingency Model in Cross-Cultural Perspective." *Leadership Theory and Research.* Eds. Marin M. Chemers and Roya Ayman. New York: Academic Press, Inc. 1993. 167–185. Print.

United States Department of Labor. "Statistics and Data: Quick Stats on Women Workers." 2009. Web. January 28, 2011.

Vinnicombe, Susan and Andrew Kakabadse. "The Debate: Do Men and Women have Different Leadership Styles?" *Manangement Focus* 12 (1999).

Weiner, Sharon Gray. "Leadership of Academic Libraries: A Literature Review." *Educational Libraries* 26.2 (2003): 5–18.

Wiegand, Wayne A. *A Biography of Melvil Dewey: Irrepressible Reformer*. Chicago: American Library Association. 1996. Print.

Winston, Mark D. "The Importance of Leadership Diversity: The Relationship between Diversity and Organizational Success in the Academic Environment." *College and Research Libraries* 62.6 (2001): 517–526.

Wolinski, Steve. "Leadership Theories." Blog: Leadership. April 2010.

4

Leadership skills

Abstract: Some of the major skills required for leaders are: motivational skills; communication skills; time-management skills; fiscal skills; and conceptual skills. Every style has its own set of skills associated with it. An autocratic leader is skilled at accomplishing tasks by demanding work from subordinates and might actually be successful in some cultures and organizations; a democratic leader is successful with his/her people skills and gets the job done. Learning and honing these skills and styles, and using them at the right time in the right place at the right level, will help leaders in their path to success.

Key words: leadership skills, time management, organizational skills, communication, cultural differences, electronic communication, critical thinking, conceptual and decision-making skills, fiscal skills, technical skills, people skills, human resources management

Motivational skills were discussed in Chapter 2. A leader's ability to be self-motivated and motivate others is not only extremely desirable, but required. Apart from motivational skills, which are indispensable in a leader, there are also other important leadership skills such as time-management, communication, conceptual or decision-making skills, critical thinking skills, fiscal skills, and people skills, along with the ability to be extremely organized.

Time management and being organized

Time management and being organized go hand in hand. Being a leader means juggling a variety of issues on any given day, all of them important to the people that are waiting for a response. In Western culture, one often hears clichés such as "time is money," "there is no time like the present," and "time is of the essence," clichés that have created a society in which "time constraints" are unlimited. Bills have to be paid on time, children have to be dropped off and picked up on time, and projects have to be completed on time – because other people involved in these activities can be affected by delays and this is not acceptable in Western culture. Librarians coming from different cultures have different senses of time. In Canada, if a person is asked to come for supper at 6 p.m., he/she is at the door at almost 6 p.m., or a few minutes after. In India, it would be considered inappropriate to arrive at the time indicated (at least in a social setting) and generally guests don't arrive for at least an hour after the scheduled time. Time is not specific and is not "urgent" in many Asian cultures. A verbal invitation for lunch or supper might just indicate that the guests come either this day or that. Anyone who watched the Commonwealth Games in September 2010 in India would have realized that "Indian time" is completely unrelated to the Western sense of time. Probably due to this, the country was unprepared on the opening day of the games. While sanitation issues and human rights issues surfaced during this time, it was also clear that due to the concept of "Indian time" the organizers and committees involved did not do enough to prepare the village for the arrival of the guests. One of the senior officials also explained that Westerners had a different idea of sanitation and that complaints were due to cultural differences (Majumder, 2010). In another example, Graham and Lam (2003) discuss the Chinese and Americans negotiating for a telecom deal. The manager of the American company (Tandem Computers) "offered to reduce the price by 5 per cent in exchange for China Telecom's commitment to sign an order for delivery within one month. The purchasing manager (of China Telecom) responded that there was no need to rush, but since the price was flexible, the price reduction would be acceptable."

On the subject of culture-specific manifestations of Indian culture, Chhokar (2007: 992) describes the context of time thus:

> There is a kind of ambivalence about time and punctuality. Whereas a number of official and business activities do occur in a present, though somewhat flexible, time frame, social activities and functions are often delayed. This ambivalence was attributed by a Western observer to language when he discovered that the word for yesterday and tomorrow in some Indian languages was the same (Kal), and therefore it did not make a difference if a meeting was held yesterday or tomorrow, for example.

Such is the concept of time in India and in many polychronic cultures where life is less structured. In "Culture and Leadership in South Africa," Booysen and Van Wyk (2007) present a study that exposes the differences in time mentality among black managers and white managers in South Africa due to differences in the perception of time as a concept. While white managers were reported to work within a linear, sequential or monochronic perception of time, black managers see time as cyclical and synchronic. For white managers, time was related to an event and therefore tangible and divisible, whereas those who see time as cyclical tend to see time commitments as desirable rather than absolute (ibid.: 465–466). Ogliastri

(2007: 699) speaks of Columbians as people who "generally arrive late for appointments (half an hour is common) although this custom has become less acceptable, and there now exists greater pressure toward being punctual, especially among companies and professionals (doctors and dentists)." In *Cultural Intelligence*, Earley and Ang (2003: 177) further confirm the fluidity of time when they say that "in the Chinese culture, it is not unusual for wedding banquets to begin two hours later than the designated schedule so that due respect is given to every single guest who took the trouble to make it to the feast." This lackadaisical attitude towards time is unacceptable in monochronic cultures such as the US, Canada, the UK and Australia. Monochronic societies are economically developed, and treat time as a scarce resource, a resource that has to be used efficiently and purposefully (Hoppe and Bhagat, 2007: 484). The Anglo-Saxon culture lives by the clock and judges people by their ability to be on time and their productivity in the time allotted. Asian, African and other polychronic cultures are more relaxed and non-linear about time. With globalization, business organizations in various countries have realized the importance of the concept of time as understood by the Western world as vital to bringing competitive advantage. They are trying to work with the Western concept of time by attempting to deliver on promised dates, but it remains a challenge.

Immigrant librarians coming from polychronic cultures should be aware of the fact that the Anglo-Saxon world runs by the clock. The calendar and clock dictate a planned and organized future. Often, meetings are scheduled a year ahead of time at timely intervals. Interviews, meetings, social gatherings all start on time and end on time. To be a successful employee, and later a leader, the cyclical sense of time has to be left behind. It is essential to be able to work with deadlines, assume multiple responsibilities within a given period, and

Figure 4.1 IQ matrix: accelerating your human potential

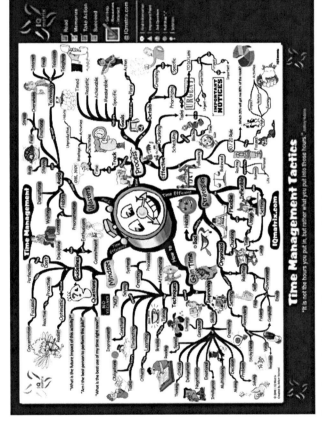

Source: from http://blog.iqmatrix.com/mind-map/time-management-mind-map

efficiently manage time in everyday work. Since time is a major organizational resource, a lack of time-management skills can cause one to lose a job or, at the very least, not to be considered for promotions. Emphasis should be on prioritizing day-to-day and long-term activities and completing projects efficiently and in a timely manner to show aptitude, adeptness, and competency. Managing time efficiently is a positive and required factor in a work environment.

In this digital era, there are many ways in which one can manage time efficiently. There are gadgets and online technologies that can send reminders. Microsoft Outlook calendars, iPad calendars, cell phones, iPhones can remind users of upcoming assignments. For those with no fancy gadgets, there are also free downloadable aids mentioned by Kumaran and Geary (2011) in their article entitled "Digital Tidbits." For the organization of work on a daily basis, one can use the digital sticky notes. Most new laptops and desktops come with downloadable sticky notes. If not, a Google search on sticky notes will provide a number of free downloadable programs. A sticky note organized by day will organize each task that needs to be accomplished on any given day, and a sticky note for the whole week gives a broader perspective on what needs to be achieved. This, along with a calendar of information, should help with time management and task completion. As emails arrive, one can also set different folders to save them. This will result in easier retrieval later. This is common knowledge for those from monochronic societies, but many from other cultures are not aware of the requirement of time-management skills as essential in order to be a successful professional.

Time management is also about the effective use of time spent on each activity. There are occasions when outside help will be required to complete a task. Recognition of this, and knowing when to seek help from the right sources, is the next step.

Figure 4.2   Time management process

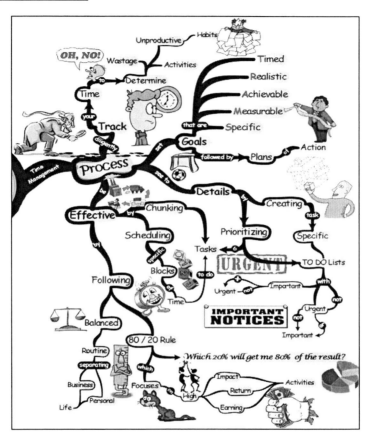

Source: from http://blog.iqmatrix.com/mind-map/time-management-mind-map

Therefore, managing time effectively entails planning, organizing, prioritizing, and executing work in a timely manner, and being flexible to accommodate last-minute changes. Proactive behavior in seeking and using modern tools or gadgets will help in accomplishing the above. Organizational skills come with practice. The more one practices, the better one gets at it.

Communication skills and cultural differences

Communication is vital for any organization. Its internal and external communications play a major role in the everyday activities that lead to success. Communication can be challenging if unclear and untimely. With cross-cultural communications there are additional challenges: information is misunderstood or lost in translation for many reasons, such as ethnocentrism, stereotyping, or confirmation bias. Ethnocentrism is when one judges others by his/her own cultural norms; stereotyping is a commonly known concept that means imposing unfair, unjust generalizations on others; confirmation bias "is the process whereby the bias is confirmed when people see what they expect to see; they are blinded to the positive attributes of others (Locker and Findley, 2009: 108). Cultures have always communicated with and understood each other based on the history between them, and individual biases. Both immigrant workers and their Anglo-Saxon cohorts need to understand the differences in cultural communications.

Edward Hall (1977) defines communication in the terms of context. He says that context and meaning are inextricably bound. He explains high-context communication as a message where information is either in the physical context or internalized in the person, where information is implicit, to be understood clearly by those within the group (or culture) but not by outsiders. Low-context cultures such as Canada, the US and many European countries value the social aspects of communication. In these cultures, it is important to communicate effectively and communicate with a purpose. Information is presented in a logical, detailed, action-oriented, and individualistic manner to inform, persuade, or build goodwill. On the other hand, many Asian and Arab cultures which are high-context cultures see the value of communication in terms of information (Locker and Findley, 2009: 108). This is perhaps the reason why high-context cultures provide information but are not overly concerned about the organization or hierarchy of the information presented. Low-context cultures use direct approaches (what you hear is what you get) and high-context cultures favor "the use of implicit and indirect messages in which meanings are embedded in the person or in the sociocultural context" (Gudykunst et al., 1996). Low-context cultures are individualistic and high-context cultures are predominantly collectivistic. These individualistic and collectivistic approaches affect the style of communication between cultures. In high-context cultures, those within the culture understand unsaid/withheld information. As Triandis observes, collectivist cultures "communicate elliptically, giving just a few clues, and letting the listener 'fill in the gaps'" and "collectivists emphasize the harmony of the relationship within the ingroup, so they do not confront, but instead use a lot of 'maybe,' 'probably,' while individualists see nothing wrong with some confrontations that will 'clear the air' and tend to use extreme terms such as 'terrific,' 'the biggest'" (Triandis, 1993: 173). In low-context cultures, information has to be clearly verbalized (or written) for others to see or understand. Minority librarians need to learn to communicate like their Anglo-Saxon cohorts and the latter should be aware of the reasons for the differences in communication from their minority cohorts. Asking questions to clarify what was communicated and how it was interpreted by all involved will help with effective communication and prevent misunderstandings on both sides. Zaidman (2011) provides an example of a cultural clash in communication between Israel and India, two very different cultures with different histories and educations.

Even though they share a common business language, English, the groups found each other to be either rude or unspecific. To quote Zaidman (ibid.), "Indian English emphasizes humility and politeness, as shown through long, indirect, and poetic sentences" while the Israelis favored a "simple and direct, even forceful" way of communicating.

However, within these cultures not every individual shares the same cultural code and therefore not everyone from a given culture communicates in a similar fashion. There are individuals within high-context cultures who prefer a direct approach and explicit messages. In any culture, the more individualistic an individual is, the more likely a preference for the use of low-context communication styles, and the more collectivistic an individual is, the more likely a preference for the use of high-context communication styles. In addition, the global economy has influenced much of the business communication to follow the ways of low-context cultures. Apart from cultural influences, individual personalities, professional experiences, and personal preferences all play a role in how one communicates.

Kinds of communication

Communication in libraries, as in many organizations, mainly takes place in three different formats: written, verbal, and non-verbal. Written communication consists of emails, memos, meeting minutes, reports, plans, and letters. Verbal communications consist of formal and informal meetings, information through the grapevine, and organizational gossip. Verbal communication takes place in meetings (face-to-face) or over the phone and this may, or may not, be followed by written minutes, depending on the formality of the meeting. Non-verbal communication uses facial expressions, body language, and gestures.

Organizations communicate (both externally and internally) in either written or verbal formats for three reasons: to inform, to persuade or request, and to build goodwill. Memos, reports, plans, and minutes usually inform; emails, letters, and meetings inform, persuade or request, or build goodwill. For the most part, Anglo-Saxon cultures and developed countries have moved away from print communication into the world of electronic communication. Many developing countries are also following suit. Nevertheless, in many of these developing countries, unlike in Western countries, written communication is not viewed in the same way as oral or electronic communication. Many oral cultures, in which printing is not necessarily the preferred or popular form of communication, have a tendency to differentiate their written and oral deliverances. As Griswold (1994: 141) explains, "oral cultures are filled with magic, enchanted with mysterious forces and spirits" and lack a clear boundary between facts and myths. On the other hand, print cultures (such as the Anglo-Saxon dominated cultures) were also literate cultures and developed the ability to differentiate between myth and history early on. There are also cultures where oral communication is as good as the written word. Therefore, a minority living in Anglo-Saxon dominated countries needs to realize that in the Western world, in formal settings, written communication should follow oral communication and both written and oral communications should convey the same message. Mean what you say and say what you mean is a common cliché in the Western world. Facts should be relayed clearly and consistently.

For immigrants who arrive in new cultures, it is going to take time to learn how to communicate effectively in verbal formats. Effective written communication is where ideas are arranged in a logical manner, in order of importance, and organized clearly by headings and subheadings, and where dates, times, and names (of those responsible for action) are mentioned when necessary. When sending emails or preparing reports, information should be relayed clearly and precisely within a described context. It is important to know email etiquette in general, and within the organizational culture. In many organizations, email is considered a formal mode of communication. In some organizational cultures, for information to be considered formal it needs to be typed and signed. Wording in written communication should be unambiguous, timely, and with a clear layout and enough white space. It should be inviting to the reader.

For those nervous about oral communication or public speaking, there is help. There are organizations such as Toastmasters International where one can learn and practice the art of communication in both written and verbal formats. Toastmasters has clubs in India, China, Afghanistan (Kabul), Malaysia, Pakistan, Singapore, many African and South American countries, Australia, the UK, the US, and Canada. Immigrants planning to migrate to their new Anglo-Saxon dominated countries may want to get an early start and visit these clubs in their own countries. Formal oral communication, just as written communication, must organize and present information in a logical and coherent manner. Whether one is communicating to inform or to persuade, it is important to speak with conviction, maintain sincere eye contact, pause in the right places, demonstrate positive body language, and not read from notes. A leader may be nervous, but this should not show when speaking in public. In oral communication, presentation aids or tools such as PowerPoint or Prezi can be used. A quick Google search for presentation aids will offer many tools that are available free of cost. Proper use of handouts and audio-visual aids will keep the audience interested and enhance the presentation.

Remembering the audience is key in communication. Depending on the audience, care should be taken not to oversimplify or over-complicate information that is being communicated. Effective communication, whether in oral or in written format, comes with lots of practice. To be an effective communicator one has to know one's strengths, weaknesses, preferences, etc. The Western world has also come up with tools that diagnose strengths and weaknesses. Personality indicator tests such as the Myers-Briggs Type Indicator are often used to examine and identify a person's behavior or style. Myers-Briggs uses four dimensions to identify people and their personalities: introvert–extrovert, sensing–judging, thinking–feeling, and perceiving–judging. Knowing where one fits in a personality indicator test can better enable a person to find their leadership style, communication style, and reasoning behaviors. While many people do not like pigeon-holing or labeling their behaviors and styles, programs such as Myers-Briggs continue to be used as a personality tester to determine characteristics of a personality. Results from these tools should only be taken as suggestions for improvement.

Along with written and verbal communication, non-verbal communication plays a significant role in communication. Non-verbal communication may take the form of gestures or body language and facial expressions, and their meanings differ across the globe. Many successful leaders pay attention to this along with other forms of communication, as words may say one thing and facial expressions may indicate another. Kirch (1979) suggests that Darwin believed that non-verbal communication, especially gestures, developed along the biological line. So, it is safe to say that non-verbal communication is born with us but is shaped by our culture.

Some gestures mean one thing in one culture and another in a different culture. The famous "uh-huh" in North America means "yes" in Canada and the US, but "no" in

India. Crossing one's arms in Western cultures indicates being closed and not interested in receiving ideas from the speaker, but in many Asian cultures such as India's, it denotes a show of respect and submissiveness. Eye contact is also interpreted differently in various cultures. While many Asian cultures do not look at a member of the opposite sex or an elderly person directly in the eye, in North America, not making eye contact is seen as a sign of dishonesty. Kirch offers other examples of these differences:

> Sticking out the tongue may be a form of mockery in the West, but in Polynesia it serves as a greeting and a sign of reverence. Clapping is our way of applauding but in Spain and the Orient it is a means of summoning the waiter. Northern Europeans usually indicate agreement by nodding their heads up and down, and shaking the head from side to side to indicate disagreement. The Greeks have for at least three thousand years used the upward nod for disagreement and the downward nod for agreement.

(Ibid.: 420).

Electronic communication

In today's globalized world, many cultures – including developing countries – have started using electronic communication as a formal mode of communication. Email is as formal as the written or typed and signed letter. While electronic communication is quick and timely, it is not always the most efficient way to communicate. But there are situations in which it is useful: sending and receiving resumes and cover letters; informing selected candidates of interview dates, times and other requirements; informing co-workers of updates in the organization, etc.

The chosen channel of communication will depend on various things: the size of the organization; the personal preferences of the communicator; the information to be communicated, etc. Depending on the importance of the message conveyed and its intended audience, the right channel should be used for the right purposes: rejections (for new positions) should not be sent via email, but via typed and signed letters. In addition, there are times when more than one channel may be used to communicate the same information.

Language and communication

Immigrants who arrive in new cultures may speak fluent English, but may not know local colloquialisms and expressions. In this global era of business, most immigrants are familiar with business English and many are masters of the language itself in its grammatical form due to their exposure to the language and their level of education, but some words or expressions can be misinterpreted or taken literally based on cultural meanings or interpretations. Native English speakers also may not understand a word that is entirely English when uttered by an immigrant. Hall (1977) describes an occasion when he was in Italy and heard the word "ferroware" used often in the business with which he was involved. It took him a while to learn that it was a newly created word for all nuts, pates and brackets made of iron or steel. The word was framed along the lines of hardware, software and firmware, words that already exist in the business world. Although, "ferroware" is an English term, it threw him completely because of the lack of context. Language has contextual meanings and emotional connotations for individuals. Even though English is a language many visible minorities are very familiar with, local expressions still might not make any sense due to lack of context. Both native English speakers and English-as-a-second-language speakers should bear this mind when communicating with each other. Communication is mutual interaction between the communicator and the receiver of the information, and this mutual interaction needs various levels of clarification.

To summarize, leaders should know how to communicate clearly so that information is complete, correct, saves time, and produces the desired effect in the reader. In cross-cultural leadership, leaders should be aware of the cultural differences in communication within verbal, non-verbal and written communications. Ask for clarifications when needed and never assume. Poor communication costs time as it takes longer to clarify information, obscures ideas, and causes confusion, it does not get the required results and undermines the image and authority of the leader. Communicating clearly, however, saves time, produces the desired effect, builds goodwill, and maintains the image of a good leader as a great communicator.

Critical thinking skills

Educational institutions from kindergarten schools to universities are focusing on these skills as something to be taught within the curriculum. What is critical thinking? Like leadership, this is another concept that cannot be defined with one or two words. It involves many things such as being open-minded, reasonable, unbiased, unassuming, asking the right questions, identifying issues before they exist, examining the credibility of sources, evaluating and synthesizing information received, being rational, self-aware, honest, and extremely disciplined. This is an important skill for a leader because leaders have to deal with lots of information, with people and with their arguments. Not all information is trustworthy or unbiased, and without the ability to filter and evaluate information leaders cannot function as effective leaders and certainly cannot lead the organization towards success. Leaders should learn not to take information at face value, but to dig deeper to find the hidden meanings or consequences of using that information. When someone tries to persuade a leader with an argument, critical thinking skills will enable the leader to "accurately interpret what they are saying or writing and evaluate whether or not they are giving a good argument ..." (Bowell and Kemp, 2005: 3). This essential skill will help a leader identify the issue being argued (or raised), deduce the necessary information from the argument in order to make decisions, evaluate that information, and conclude with results or create a process for achieving results. *Logos*, or logic, is the important aspect in critical thinking skills, because logical fallacy can lead to polarization – trying to force one to believe that there are only two possible options, only one of which is acceptable; or blindering – limiting options unnecessarily even when aware of other options (Locker and Findley, 2009: 7). Leaders with critical thinking skills will find more than two options and many ways to work with these options. With critical thinking skills, information is already available. On the other hand, having conceptual skills means an abiblity to deal with abstracts.

Conceptual and decision-making skills

Conceptual skills refer "to a person's ability to think in the abstract, to diagnose and analyse different situations" (Griffin et al., 2011: 188). It is the ability to connect separate concepts or ideas and create a bigger picture; the ability to find the relationship between individual concepts and connect them to a framework to make the best decisions; the ability to come up with creative strategies and solutions before the problem starts. Often a leader is in a situation where there are no facts or evidence upon which to base decisions. In such situations, a leader is expected to make the best possible ingenious and applicable decisions based on experience, the sparse information available, and by being a visionary. Decision-making is a process of finding alternatives and choosing the alternative that works best for the organization and its employers. It is not about being coldly objective in order to produce results. A leader with good conceptual and decision-making skills has the ability to identify potential partners for the organization to provide both moral and financial support. In a library setting, a leader who can identify potential partners at an early stage starts to build relationships, finds new ways of improving library services, and offers better programs and efficient workspaces. In an economic downturn, many countries, even the developed ones, consider shutting down libraries or some library services to save money. This is one situation where a leader's conceptual skills may save the library, its employees, and users.

When enough information is available a SWOT analysis can be used: to identify the Strengths and Weaknesses of the organization; and the Opportunities and Threats that need to be identified before making a decision. There are many demands and time and money constraints on a leader, and good conceptual skills will help in choosing the right options that will meet those demands and stay within any constraints. As mentioned in the previous chapters, leaders, at least in the library world, no longer have to make decisions without consulting their cohorts. But it is imperative that the leader who has the bigger picture of the organization is able to guide the group's decision-making process to fit the goals of the organization in the long run, and this cannot be done without conceptual or basic decision-making skills.

Fiscal skills

Many of the decisions a leader makes may involve money management. Offering library programs, creating a new librarian or staff position and hiring for that position, providing training, allowing a library employee to be away at conferences, training, providing research funding or sabbaticals, all cost money. Hence, managing money is also an important skill for leaders. After establishing external relationships, a leader has to show how effectively he or she can run the organization by making the right decisions based on many things, but most importantly based on the money spent by the organization. Learning to budget and knowing how to spend money effectively shows that the leader is being financially responsible. It is not a bad idea for anyone in a leadership position to take a course in managerial and/or financial accounting, so that they understand how money is spent both internally and externally to help with decision-making.

Managerial accounting, also known as cost accounting, helps internal decision-makers. Jones et al. (2003: 2) define it as "the process of identification, measurement, accumulation, analysis, preparation, interpretation and communication of financial information used by management to plan, evaluate, and control an organization." Although a leader may not be directly involved in spending funds for collections and pay checks etc., a leader is finally accountable for anything that happens with these funds. If a library declares a lack of funds and does not improve its collections or hire new staff, the leader shares the blame for not managing monies appropriately.

Financial accounting is collecting, recording, and presenting financial information to external agencies such as the government, shareholders, and creditors. This is a mandatory accounting exercise in all organizations as it is important to be accountable to all external partnerships.

Every organization has goals. Many involve financial commitments. In a library setting, adding to the physical or electronic collection or hiring new staff, including librarians, are examples of goals that cost money. Organizations set their goals with the help of strategic planning – a long-range plan that outlines actions to be taken in order to achieve the set goals. Libraries, like many organizations, typically have 3–5-year strategic plans that complement their parent organization's strategic plans. For example, a university library will have a strategic plan that is built around the university's strategic plan and a school library will have a strategic plan that supports the school's or school board's strategic plan.

A good strategic plan involves input from all essential partners, provides a timeframe, lays out the action plans, sets objectives to be achieved, and details the personnel who will undertake or lead these actions. This clear planning helps an organization set aside money, time, and staff to achieve its goals. A leader may not be involved in every step of this strategic plan but has responsibility for the outcome of the plan. An efficient plan can be put together by a leader who has an understanding of the availability of present and future funds for the organization.

A leader should be knowledgable about the organization's operating and capital budget. Again, the dean or the director of a library is not necessarily involved in the day-to-day operating budget (delivery trucks, inter-library loan charges, fines paid, electricity bills, etc.) nor the long-term capital budget expenses (buying self-checkout machines, a new library building, new land for the library) but will have a major input in the decision-making process of what and where to buy. Without being aware of the funding situation, a leader cannot make the right decisions on how to proceed. Leaders should also learn to be financial managers and manage cash flow, assume financial control, and be involved in financial planning even if they are not directly involved with the money. In today's economy financial planning is important for libraries. A financial plan "describes a firm's strategies for reaching some future financial position" (Griffin et al., 2011: 654), and libraries are constantly trying to find ways to fund their projects via outside environments.

In many cultures, women are not the money managers in their families. Men have control of the money and women librarians coming from these cultures may not be comfortable with handling large amounts of money. It is beneficial to take basic lessons on money management, management accounting, and accounting practices, and learn from the financial manager of the institution, colleagues, and mentors.

Technical skills

To communicate effectively and get everyday work done in a timely manner, leaders need to be technically astute as well. Technology is ubiquitous and ever-changing. No one, including the leader, is expected to know how to use every type of technology that comes their way (e.g., iPad, iPhone, wiki, blogs, etc.), but leaders should be able to adapt to and learn new technology quickly. They should be proactive in learning to use new tools. As a leader, it is important not to be technically handicapped or dependent on others. Being aware of new technologies and learning to use them can help a leader keep in touch with others and allow for the fast and efficient flow of information, which can save time and money.

Many libraries, especially public and school libraries, are slow in using emerging technologies due to a lack of funds. Many academic and college libraries provide the funds, resources, and training for buying and using the latest technologies. Websites such as YouTube also offer free demonstrations on how to use some of the new technologies in the market. In many cases a new technological tool can be learnt by doing (especially helpful when available free of cost). A leader might have to create a presentation, write a speech, or schedule meetings. Knowing the right tool to use and knowing how to create a presentation can make the information clear and even influential. It is understandable that some of the ethnic minorities may not be familiar with all the technologies of the developed world, but a willingness to learn is key.

Human relations skills (or people skills)

Skillful human relations is the ability to get along with other people, and this cannot be achieved without empathy, good communication skills, and an understanding of the diversity that exists: diversity in people's behavior, cultures, gender, age, beliefs, religious, educational, and socio-economic backgrounds. Human relations is different from human resources skills. Human resources is a "set of organizational skills directed at attracting, developing, and maintaining an effective workforce" (ibid.: 242). While it is important to have a stable human resources plan in order to find, hire, and keep an effective workforce, a good leader should also possess human relations skills in order to maintain and sustain a productive workforce.

As Mullins and Linehan (2005: 137) explain, "The ability to get on with people, at all levels, would be one of the main qualities required of any library leader, and this includes relating with the pubic, with library staff, and with management staff of the local authority." They also go on to say that having good people skills means having good communication skills, good listening skills, and being a good talker. A leader without human relations skills has no understanding of the needs of his or her employees and is therefore incapable of empathizing with and motivating employees to achieve their fullest potential both individually and collectively for the organization's success. Lack of human relation skills in a leader can cause high turnover, break goodwill among internal and external organizational partners, and eventually contribute to the failure of the organization.

Lately, a skill that has been identified as very important is that of reflective practice. This is the ability to stop and think critically about what one is doing. Lambert (2003: 6) defines it as "the genesis of innovation." Literature on reflective practice identifies this skill as a crucial way to understand oneself, and one which will enable a better understanding of others. The idea of the importance of this skill is not new but is gaining momentum again. In 1984, Kolb popularized the relationship between reflection and learning. Schön (1987) explains reflection as:

> Diagnosis, testing and belief in personal causation. Diagnosis is the ability to frame or make sense of a problem through use of professional knowledge, past experience, the uniqueness of the setting and the people involved, and expectations held by others. Once framed, the reflective practitioner engages in on-the-spot experimentation and reflection to test alternative solutions.

Libraries are dynamically changing organizations that strive to meet the demands of their communities with information and technology. Library leaders work under a constant challenge of being able to meet these demands, and can easily get held up in "doing" something and forget to think about the process: the before and after. Reflecting on the before and after will shed light on the gaps that can be filled, other external factors that needed to be assessed, and the long-term implications of decisions.

In any given organization, there are people with different skills and abilities. A leader with good human resources skills should be able to identify these skills and capitalize on them. Getting to know one's employees, their work preferences, any personal problems (that they are willing to share) that might be affecting their performance, will help a leader understand and relate to each of the employees differently. In the case of ethnic minorities who come from different countries, there could be lots of personal issues: a lack of friends and family nearby, feelings of homesickness, and in some cases lack of money, are some of the issues that could be bothering them in their everyday lives. Many do not get the chance to visit their families often and anything that might be happening in their birth country could be affecting their performance. In cross-cultural leadership this is an important factor to consider. In order to avoid major setbacks due to personal problems it helps to clarify the role of each employee within the organization, and to set clear goals for performance on a timely basis both for individual employees and for the organization as a whole. As mentioned above, strategic plans can be used when defining personal goals for employees.

To conclude, leaders need to possess many skills and know how to use the right one in the right situation. Leadership is a learning process and good leaders are dynamic. To quote Mullins and Linehan again: "Personal qualities are not fixed within individuals as they can change through influence, continued education, training, experience, as well as fluctuating within individuals, such as changing personal circumstances, or the impact of mentors and other colleagues" (Mullins and Linehan, 2005: 134).

Learning and building these skills, and being adaptive to changes, will pave the way to becoming a good leader and enable the leader to nurture, have an insight into employee issues, and be innovative with problem solving and decision-making. Once good foundational skills are built, efforts should be taken to maintain and acquire more skills – exploring the unknown. Humility, self-awareness, and a willingness to adapt will all help in one's journey towards leadership.

References

Booysen, Lize A. E. and Marius W. van Wyk. "Culture and Leadership in South Africa." *Culture and Leadership Across the World: The Globe Book of In-Depth Studies of 25 Societies.* Eds. Jagdeep S. Chhokar, Felix C. Brodbeck and Robert J. House. Mahwah, New Jersey: Lawrence Erlbaum Associates. 2007. 433–474. Print.

Bowell, Tracy and Gary Kemp. *Critical Thinking: A Concise Guide.* London: Taylor & Francis. 2005.

Chhokar, Jagdeep S. "India: Diversity and Complexity in Action." *Culture and Leadership Across the World: The Globe Book of In-Depth Studies of 25 Societies.* Eds. Jagdeep S. Chhokar, Felix C. Brodbeck and Robert J. House. Mahwah, New Jersey: Lawrence Erlbaum Associates. 2007. 971–1020. Print.

Earley, Christopher P. and Soon Ang. *Cultural Intelligence: Individual Interactions Across Cultures.* Stanford: Stanford University Press. 2003. Print.

Edwards, George. "It's OK, They All Speak English." *European Business Review* 90.3 (1990): 8–12. Print.

Graham, John L. and N. Mark Lam. "The Chinese Negotiation." *Harvard Business Review* (October 2003): 82–91.

Griffin, Ricky W. et al. *Business.* Toronto: Pearson Canada. 2011. Print.

Griswold, Wendy. *Cultures and Societies in a Changing World.* Thousand Oaks: Pine Forge Press. 1994. Print.

Gudykunst, William B., Yuko Matsumoto, Stella Ting-Toomey, Tsukasa Nishida, Kwangsu Kim and Sam Heyman. "The Influence of Cultural Individualism-Collectivism, Self Construals, and Individual Values on Communication Styles across Cultures." *Human Communication Research* 22.4 (1996): 510–543. Print.

Hall, Edward T. *Beyond Culture.* Toronto: Random House of Canada. 1977. Print.

Hoppe, Michael H. and Rabi S. Bhagat. "Leadership in the United States of America: The Leader as a Cultural Hero." *Culture and Leadership Across the World: The Globe Book of In-Depth Studies of 25 Societies.* Eds. Jagdeep S. Chhokar, Felix C. Brodbeck and Robert J. House. Mahwah, New Jersey: Lawrence Erlbaum Associates. 2007. 474–543. Print.

Jones, Kumen H., Michael L. Werner, Katherine P. Terrell, Robert L. Terrell and Peter R. Norwood. *Introduction to Management Accounting.* Toronto: Prentice Hall. 2003. Print.

Kirch, Max S. "Non-Verbal Communication Across Cultures." *The Modern Language Journal* 63.8 (1979): 416–423. Print.

Kolb, David A. *Experiential Learning*. Englewood Cliffs: Prentice Hall. 1984. Print.

Kumaran, Maha and Joe Geary. "Digital Tidbits." *Computers in Libraries* 31.1 (2011): 11–15, 38–39. Print.

Lambert, Linda. "Leadership Redefined: An Evocative Context for Teacher Leadership." *School Leadership and Management* 23.4 (2003): 421–430.

Locker, Kitty and Isobel Findley. *Business Communication Now*. Canada: McGraw Hill Ryerson. 2009. Print.

Majumder, Sanjoy. *Commonwealth Games: India Vows to Fix Delhi Village*. September 2010. Web. February 14, 2011.

Mullins, John and Margaret Linehan. "Desired Qualities of Public Library Leaders." *Leadership and Organization Development Journal* 27.2 (2005): 133–143.

Ogliastri, Enrique. "Colombia: The Human Relations Side of Enterprise." *Culture and Leadership Across the World: The Globe Book of In-Depth Studies of 25 Societies*. Eds. Jagdeep S. Chhokar, Felix C. Brodbeck and Robert J. House. Mahwah, New Jersey: Lawrence Erlbaum Associates. 2007. 689–722. Print.

Schön, Donald A. *Educating the Reflective Practitioner: Toward a New Design for Teaching and Learning in the Professions*. San Francisco: Jossey-Bass. 1987. Print.

Triandis, Harry C. "The Contingency Model in Cross-Cultural Perspective." *Leadership Theory and Research: Perspectives and Directions*. Eds. Martin M. Chemers and Roya Ayman. New York: Academic Press, Inc. 1993. 167–185. Print.

Zaidman, Nurit. "Cultural Codes and Language Strategies in Business Communication." *Management of Communication Quarterly* 14.3 (2011): 408–441.

5

Leadership in school, public, and academic libraries in the US, the UK, Canada and Australia

Abstract: School, public, and academic libraries are the focus of this chapter. While all three library sectors have always had funding issues, and more so now since the 2008 economic crunch, school and public libraries are the most affected by budgets with regard to staff, collections, and technology upgrades. These are the two sectors that either close their doors permanently or stay open with reduced hours and fewer services. It is also these two sectors in which leadership literature is in short supply. From the leadership literature available, it is evident that all three library sectors are interested in doing something or other to improve their libraries and, most importantly, also interested in doing something towards building leadership in their libraries in spite of the political and economic issues.

Key words: school library leadership, public library leadership, leadership programs, academic library leadership, Aurora leadership, Minnesota Institute, Spectrum Scholarship, Leadership and Career Development Program, Association of Research Libraries

Much of the literature available on library leadership, regardless of the sector (public, school, or academic) focuses on the lack of leadership initiatives and the issue of librarians still being hesitant about leadership in libraries. In 2001, Riggs challenged librarians to name three library articles with leadership in their titles (ibid.: 8). In the same year Glegoff (2001: 79) worried that "without skillful leadership from library administrators to pilot a course through the enormous challenges" it is doubtful "that libraries will retain the esteem traditionally held for them by the public." In 2005, Mullins and Linehan found librarians in their survey articulating that "many head librarians are not making that changeover from librarians to leaders" (ibid.: 392) and that "leadership never featured highly in librarianship before" (ibid.). In 2003, the Demos article found that "leadership was the most frequently cited development need identified in the stakeholder interviews" (ibid.: 19). In the same year, Black found that some of the major library databases retrieved depressing results on a search of leadership. He speaks of Proquest, Expanded Academic Index, Australian Library and Information Science Abstracts (ALISA), the Australian Library Journal (ALJ) and the Australian Computer Society (ACS) (Black, 2003: 454–455). It is even more depressing to try and find anything on ethnic-minority leadership. More articles and books have been written on leadership for librarians since Riggs' challenge, but there is the question of whether it is being practiced. As Riggs says, since "there is no more powerful engine driving a library toward excellence and success than its leadership" (Riggs, 1998: 8) so librarians from all sectors need to focus on leadership issues for their organizations.

Acree et al. (2001) speak of the under-representation of librarians and give some reasons as to why. Minorities are frustrated with the glass ceiling in the profession and feel marginalized because they are hired at entry-level positions and there is a lack of movement beyond that. He cites Howland (1999) who pointed out the problem. The problem was not in hiring minorities into the profession but in helping them move ahead by recognizing their skills and potential. This problem has its roots in library schools. There are not enough minority students in library schools and therefore not enough to enter the profession. And when they leave out of frustration there are even less of them available for leadership positions. With first generation immigrants, their education from within their home countries is not always recognized, which only makes it more challenging and frustrating for them to enter the library profession.

School libraries and leadership

In the US, a library service to schools began around the 1800s when book wagons delivered books to schools (Michie and Holton, 2005: 2). It wasn't until Congress passed the Elementary and Secondary Education Act (ESEA) of 1965 that money was set aside for school libraries and only then were libraries viewed as an integral part of schools (ibid.: 3). The launch of Sputnik by Russia caused an urgency in creating better schools and out of this evolved the concept of good school libraries staffed by proper personnel. But both then and now school libraries have had to compete for funding at the local and state levels with many other programs. As Hopkins and Butler (1991: 34) state, "although many school library media programs received funding in the consolidated laws, the consolidation of education programs ended the consistent growth of library media programs throughout the nation." But in 2002, the US Congress decided to dedicate $250 million "funding for school library materials to get its school libraries back on track" (Haycock, 2003: 3).

In the UK, research on school library leadership focuses on a similar issue as in the US: the ability to create (or in some cases keep) an integrated library, a learning center for the school and the community. There are budget, collection, and staff issues. The strategic report by Streatfield et al. (2010) outlines these issues in school libraries in the present day UK. This report identified that many libraries did not have a policy in place (ibid.: 13), many libraries do not operate a full school day (ibid.: 31), the library stock does not grow proportionately to the growth in student numbers, and almost 30 per cent of school libraries have "fewer than 10 [computer] machines available for students in the library" (ibid.: 35). The report also highlights the importance of a reporting structure for libraries in schools: "who the librarian reports to can be viewed as an indicator of how the school views its library. 405 of the respondents (38.8 per cent) report to the Head or Deputy Head ... but 105 (10 per cent) report to the Bursar, Finance Director or Business Manager, which is likely to weaken the librarian's scope for engaging with curriculum matters."

In Australia, too, school libraries have struggled for survival. There have been suggestions that they work with public libraries, not only to ensure survival, but to provide continuous learning, to provide access to more users, and to continue to be educational laboratories for all students. In spite of the many reports that shed light on the limitations of school and children's library services in Australia since 1964, the trend continues (Bundy, 2002). The National Institute of Quality Teaching and School Leadership in Australia was established in 2004 to raise the status, quality, and professionalism of teachers and school leaders throughout Australia. The Australian School Library Association (ASLA) and the Australian Library and Information Association (ALIA) together formed a partnership to address common priorities in schools and libraries. This included "articulating and promoting the role of library and information services and staff within the school community" (Mitchell, 2006: 42).

Bundy's suggestion is joint-use libraries, where public and school libraries cooperate in a formal way to fill the gaps in services and collections, and to provide a continuum for a student researcher/learner from school to public library to college or academic library as they progress into adulthood. The 2003 article published by Demos also suggests that different kinds of libraries and museums have commonalities. The article goes on to say that "there are great areas of overlap where the domains can come together to improve their performance" (ibid.: 18). Joint-venture libraries exist in Canada too and the most common of these is the school/public library (Wilson, 2008).

In 2003, Haycock released an executive summary of the state of school libraries in Canada, in which he stated that US researchers found a direct correlation between test scores or better performance at university or college levels and having a full-time teacher librarian in US schools. Haycock observed that no such study had been carried out in Canada and spoke of the decline in the state of the school library when he said, "only 10 per cent of Ontario elementary schools have a full-time teacher-librarian, compared with 42 per cent twenty-five years ago ..." (ibid.: 6). Other provinces didn't fare well either. In 2011, he confirmed that well-stocked, well-staffed school libraries do make a difference to student learners by creating an interest in reading and providing high-quality learning. School library leadership literature focuses on niche leadership issues. This is perhaps due to the constant threat to budgets and staffing. The ESEA mentions leadership in school libraries only in relation to "selecting, acquiring, organizing, and using instructional materials" (Michie and Holton, 2005: 4). Academic and public libraries focus on these niche leadership issues as well, but with both of them, especially the academic libraries, there is a need for someone to lead the organization as a whole and, therefore, the leadership research focuses on the leaders' experience, expertise, and overall efficiency.

In school library leadership literature, there are papers on being visionary leaders, literacy leaders, or transformational leaders to be prepared for the "worst of times." And these papers focus on being able to build or keep a collection with creative problem solving by being visionaries, and transformational leaders. Smith (2010) focuses on transformational leadership in school libraries and her focus is on the one most important skill librarians would require to become efficient transformational leaders – technology. Although Smith's paper focuses only on 30 pre-service school library media specialists from six Florida counties and the impact of their technology training on transformational technology, it is clear that a lack of current technology and/ or a lack of knowledge of current technology is an issue in many school libraries. Oberg (2010) refers to technology as a "daunting challenge" for school librarians. She quotes other authors who challenge librarians to understand and respect the world of video-gamers and their ways of learning. Dow (2010) speaks of transformational and transactional leadership as necessary for school librarians who are (or should be) information and technology literacy leaders. Coatney (2011) writes of being prepared for leadership during hard times when there is no budget for new acquisitions; maintaining collections and staffing for school libraries and library programs through "creativity, compassion, and collaboration to reach the ultimate goals" (ibid.: 38). A similar vein runs through Johns' (2011) article in which she refers to the 4 Cs of leadership as "Communication, Collaboration, Critical thinking and problem solving, and Creativity and Innovation," in that order. Achterman (2010) focuses on how to be a literacy leader by "gain[ing] a deep understanding of the reading and writing processes, of the best practices for teaching literacy skills across the curriculum, of the role technology plays in literacy instruction and learning, and of best practices in the ways school librarians contribute to student literacy gains." School librarians need to be proactive in their leadership roles by approaching teachers and administrators with new ideas for incorporating research skills into the school curriculum. They need to be proactive in teaching administrators and teachers that their library is more than a warehouse for books.

Apart from the challenges of funding and issues related to it, school librarians, in spite of being in a teaching environment, also do not have an evaluative function. Academic librarians teach classes on using library resources and there is therefore an evaluative aspect to their role. Many academic librarians are expected to publish and this makes them researchers and self-evaluators. But in most school libraries library usage is not part of the curriculum, and while students are encouraged to use the library, they are not evaluated on their knowledge of the intricacies of catalog searches or the difference between using a database and Google for searches. Mitchell (2006) highlights a significant debate caused by the inclusion of the phrase "evaluate student learning" in the Standards of Professional Excellence for Teacher Librarians in 2005. Many teacher librarians did not see this as their role. Since school libraries form the foundation for learning, having a well-established school library where student users are not only taught but also evaluated for their active library learning will create an enlightened student population when they move to universities and colleges. Coatney (2011) sees this as an opportunity to establish leadership in school libraries. She speaks of leadership in terms of collaboration: constantly learning, relying on others, working hard to honor all learners, and determining what is best for a student as a learner (ibid.: 40).

A school librarian has to be proactive in taking on or creating new projects that will establish the library and its resources, along with the librarian's services, at the center of the curriculum. Without proper leadership, school libraries become models of servitude rather than places of learning.

Lack of applications from school librarians

Jones (2011) quotes Peter Bromberg, one of the program facilitators of the Emerging Leaders Program, on selecting applicants for the program as saying, "we do not want an overwhelming percentage of emerging leaders to be academic librarians for example and sacrifice special librarians and school media librarians." Whether this implies that there are so many academic librarians applying for the program that school media librarians do not get a chance at this leadership program is not clear. But the shortage of school librarians in a position to apply for the program is a concern. The ALA page on Emerging Leader Participants for 2011 does not specify whether the participants are from school, public, or academic libraries, but judging from the sponsors there are five school librarians in the program. The lack of interest from school librarians for participation in a leadership program, or their inability to commit six months, or any length of time, to a leadership program during their working year is a challenge. Even a program set within a virtual learning environment is a challenge as many school librarians are solo librarians or the only personnel in their library. Winston and Neely (2001), in their research on the Snowbird Leadership program, identified that most of the applicants were either from public libraries (44 per cent) or academic libraries (16.66 per cent).

In a school library situation, the principal's support in establishing and maintaining a good library is of the utmost importance. If the leadership at the principal's level is not receptive to innovative ideas for the school library (or even for keeping the school library), then there is a problem. Supporting a library includes hiring librarians rather than having existing teachers take on the librarian's role, providing technology support for librarians, including library research as part of the curriculum (this may have to be worked out with the school board), improving technology, and keeping up with technology trends. Libraries should not be seen as warehouses for information keeping, but places of reading, learning, sharing, and distributing information. It doesn't help when fewer than 7 per cent of principals in Arizona believe that "school library media specialists should exercise leadership roles in the educational community" (Hartzell, 2002: 93). So in cases where principals are not aware of the library's importance, existing teacher librarians should take on the leadership role in enlightening principals and the school community. Having said that, it is also encouraging to know that in the last two decades or so researchers in education have begun challenging the "pervasive view that equates school leadership with principalship" (Foster, 2005: 35). Saunders' (2011) article highlights the importance of leadership through instruction and states, "teacher leaders understand the political landscape of the institution and organizations within which they function, know where the power bases lay and understand how to act strategically within this framework" (ibid.: 268). Teachers can be leaders.

While there is some literature on leadership in school libraries, there is a lack of literature on ethnic-minority leadership in school libraries in the UK, the US, Canada, and Australia.

Public libraries and leadership

Public libraries have established leadership in many areas in the past – information literacy, joint-use libraries, interdisciplinary collections (something for everyone), computer literacy, free computers for public use, multicultural collections, multilingual collections, special services for homebound seniors, etc. – but research shows that many public libraries, at least in the US and Canada, are unprepared when it comes to future leadership. Public libraries owe their birth and existence to many like William Ewart, Andrew Carnegie, and Melvil Dewey for the roles they played in creating and establishing public libraries, and to all the supporters of knowledge who created a structure and a place for libraries and considered knowledge to be a public property to be available free of charge. William Ewart sponsored the Public Libraries Act of 1850, fighting the Conservatives to do so, and finally managed to pass a bill after many modifications that portrayed public libraries as having a reformative role rather than an educational role. Ewart and supporters of this bill saw public libraries "as a counter-agent to evils rather than as a positive force for educational or recreational benefit" (Max, 1984: 504), and Ewart firmly believed in education as the "great preventative measure" against crime (ibid.: 507). Later public libraries were seen as places of knowledge, where information was available for free. They also began to evolve as social spaces, with programs for children, young adults and adults, and multicultural groups. In spite of a library's usefulness and immediate relevance to the community, every once in a while there is an economic crisis that threatens its existence. In the UK, "The Public Libraries Act 1964 still provides the national statutory framework and the general context for local service delivery by local authorities, who are the accountable bodies" (Daines, 2009). At the time of writing this chapter, one of the biggest issues being discussed among UK librarians on the public library list serve via CILIP was the announcement by the Mayor of Newham, Sir Robin Wales, to remove all multilingual newspapers from libraries so as to encourage immigrants to learn English. With over 150 languages spoken by the residents of this London borough who use its library, this is, to say the least, the worst leadership move a Mayor can make (BBC, May 10, 2011). It takes the library and its users a few steps backward. One of the ways to integrate new immigrants into a society is by providing information in a language they understand and are most comfortable with. This will help with the social inclusion of new immigrants. Without information new immigrants cannot integrate into their new societies, and this will cause a major disturbance in the social fabric of multicultural societies such as England. The difference between informational "haves" and "have-nots" creates a major disparity among citizens of a society and this contributes to differences in their economic and educational possibilities, which does not contribute towards a knowledgable, self-sustaining society. As Caidi and Allard explain:

> To stifle individual expression or attempt to subsume it under a repressive notion of social cohesion may be what leads to the disruption of the social fabric. An imposed homogeneity for the sake of a false notion of sameness may in fact be what encourages social alienation, isolation, and exclusion.

> (Caidi and Allard, 2005: 311)

In Canada, lending institutions have existed for more than 200 years and each province and territory has its own library act and a system that mandates its funding, partnerships (Wilson, 2008), and therefore its staffing and collections. Public library history in Australia was established after the Library Bill was passed in 1939. Prior to that, libraries existed as subscription reading rooms. The Munn-Pitt Report of 1935 stated that Australian libraries were "wretched little institutes" and "cemeteries of old and forgotten books." These libraries were run by untrained staff, with limited public access. The release of this report was the catalyst for the establishment of Free Libraries, as they exist in Australia today. They were established as government-funded services and continue to be so today (Berryman, 2004). There are over 1,500 public libraries in Australia, although not all of them have all the necessary facilities or services, for a number of reasons such as the lack of a network for internet access. This resulted in the establishment of Public Libraries Australia (PLA) in 2002, before which there was no national body to represent the Australian public libraries. Since then the PLA has served as the voice of the public libraries at the national level by providing advocacy and support, by lobbying the government for funding in Australia, and by being the single point of contact for the Federal Government on matters of online accessibility (Makin and Knight, 2006). Bundy (1999) wants librarians to go back to the idea that libraries are about reading, not information retrieval. Of all three library sectors, this thinking can be best applied to public libraries where users come to read for pleasure or to gain knowledge. Bundy's tone indicates that librarians (and library users) are now techno-lusts and that they should return to promoting reading as the catalyst for public libraries to thrive. He argues that public libraries are used by 11.4 million Australians, comparing this to the 30,000 or so students at a university setting in Melbourne or Sydney. Perhaps it is the lack of perspective that public library leadership needs to focus on.

In the current economic climate, public libraries, too, are struggling to stay open, in the same way as are school libraries. Libraries have become the first target when funding is an issue, and smaller libraries in many communities in the US have had to close their doors. The closure of public libraries is also a major concern in the UK (McMenemy, 2009). In England and Wales, 179 service points were closed between 1986–1997 due to financial, structural, contractual, and low-usage reasons (Proctor and Simmons, 2000). Davies (2008) observes that the Conservative Government single-handedly caused a decline in library usage through insufficient funding, lack of partnerships, lack of training, and the de-skilling of libraries by hiring lay staff and volunteers instead of librarians. He blames this Government for the actions that pushed the "library service into the orbit of private sector and changed irrevocably the character of the service" (ibid.: 4). Stewart (2011) reports that 375 public libraries across the UK could soon face closure.

During a recession, there is an inflation of prices on books and other information packages and public libraries are often unable to add to their collections. Jobs may also be cut and, due to shortages in personnel, maintaining collections and offering other services becomes a challenge. Ironically, the same reason, an economic crunch, can also be a reason for an increased usage of library materials. Rooney-Brown (2009) provides evidence of a connection between an increase in the usage in libraries across the US and the economic downturn in his article, and confirms that there is a "growing body of statistical and anecdotal evidence which supports the theory that there is indeed a link between public library usage and economic crises" (ibid.: 342). Davies (2008) confirms this by stating that in 2006–2007 more people in the UK visited libraries than either football matches or the cinema.

Leadership literature on public libraries shows the lack of preparation on the part of public libraries when it comes to succession planning. As Mullins and Linehan (2005) found, many public librarians in Ireland and Britain stated that "library chiefs do not have a mental picture of themselves as real managers or leaders" and that they are "books people, not leaders," but all agreed that libraries need effective leadership (ibid.: 392). Many public libraries also do not have strategies in place for finding the right leadership for the future of their library. Succession planning should not be about finding a replacement when a person retires. It should be about mentoring all existing librarians and identifying the right person for the right leadership positions that may come along at any given time. Librarians who are identified as potential leaders should be involved in succession planning. This will provide motivation and help with retention. As Whitmell (2011) explains, individuals should not be identified for specific positions or advancement without discussion with the individuals involved to be sure that they want the job and are willing to undertake the needed training and coaching to get there. The plan must be flexible and adaptable to change. Individuals identified for leadership positions should be from different cultural backgrounds.

What are public libraries doing about ethnic-minority leadership?

In the UK, CILIP published its Encompass Toolkit (2009) offering guidance and advice to library and information organizations to undertake positive action training initiatives. This report highlights the importance of cultural diversity among library employees and offers ideas on how to conduct training programs, what supervisors and trainers need to be aware of during training, and the dos and don'ts of such a program. This training program is meant to offer well-rounded career development advice about the library field without making assumptions about the trainee's choices. In Canada, the Canadian Library Association (CLA) speaks only of the provision of multicultural services and collections to users and nothing of hiring minority librarians in the various sectors. The CLA's position statement explains, "The Canadian Library Association believes that a diverse and pluralistic society is central to our country's identity. Libraries have a responsibility to contribute to a culture that recognizes diversity and fosters social inclusion." The Public Library Association (PLA) of the US, a division of the ALA, also has nothing on hiring public librarians at their libraries, but refers to the ALA for its diversity issues, which covers topics such as combating racism, library education to meet the needs of a diverse society, the recruitment and retention of diverse personnel, and leadership development and advancement for diverse librarians. At the time of researching for this book, there was nothing to be found within the Public Libraries Australia (PLA) or the Australian Library and Information Association (ALIA) regarding hiring and retaining diverse librarians, and the author's emails to the PLA on the matter went unanswered.

Leadership programs for public librarians

Most public libraries do not offer their own leadership programs and often rely on other sources in their community or library organizations for such programs. Some of the community programs may not be tailored for librarians and this could pose a challenge. In some cases, librarians may have to travel to different places to complete their leadership workshops and this is not always a feasible option for many. It is left up to the librarians in these programs to learn, synthesize, and apply their newly acquired leadership knowledge to their own work environments. The benefit of what is learnt in these programs will wear off if not practiced within a supportive environment within the library, and this is another challenge for public librarians. Having the time to practice learnt leadership skills in a supportive environment is a luxury that most public librarians cannot afford due to a lack of staffing and funding, etc. Since leadership programs cost money, librarians at public libraries mostly go to one or two short-term leadership programs and this alone is not a good learning opportunity. Public librarians should also remember that leadership is not just about attending leadership workshops or becoming members of various library associations, but applying what is learnt at these workshops and using the skills learnt from being members of library associations in their work environment. Public libraries need to create a supportive environment for those identified as potential candidates for leadership. And these candidates should be chosen from diverse backgrounds and cultures with diverse knowledge to truly represent the community they serve.

Public librarians have relied on peer-mentorship to learn their jobs and develop leadership skills. Gail Doherty (2006) warns that while this is commendable it can also lead to clashes of style: younger librarians are more comfortable with technology and may have different communication styles and approaches to objectives. Older librarians may be reluctant to use technology and may have a different perspective on their work. But leadership learning and practice involves going beyond one's comfort zones and learning to work with various styles and skill sets in different people.

How can leadership help public librarians?

It is encouraging to know that libraries are well used, especially so during a recession, and public library leaders need to focus on leadership to acquire funding to maintain their library. Since libraries enhance the lives of ordinary people and create informed citizens, this is an important task for public library leaders to consider. Mullins and Linehan (2005) highlight the need for political skills among library leaders, an important skill since libraries rely on the support of politicians for resources. They say, "political skills and political correctness are also needed to deal successfully with management and especially senior management" (ibid.: 137). In the absence of a school library, a public library is one of the few places young users can go to get free information. Finding and forming partnerships, using fiscal and technology skills to provide as many services and programs as possible, using communication skills to let government bodies know how valuable the library is for a community, making the library a hub of the community by working with various groups, schools and even local colleges and universities, all require creative leadership. Finding funding is not an easy task for public libraries anywhere, but finding those funds and using them wisely makes one a good leader. Good leadership will create libraries that can flow with change, manage change, and accommodate new ideas in order to maintain successful libraries of the future. Good leadership should be about finding ways to take libraries beyond their fight for survival with every economic downturn.

Leadership in academic libraries

Similar to school libraries, but unlike public libraries, academic libraries speak of leadership in terms of instruction. As discussed previously, school librarians do not have an evaluative role in their instruction but academic librarians do. Hence, instruction is seen as an integral part of the academic librarian's job. Providing good instruction means that librarians constantly work on developing their professional skills through continuing education, research, workshops, and training. Leadership in academic libraries can be established in technology, research skills, mobile resources, etc. With so many disciplines on campus in any given academic library, leadership for librarians and library staff can expand across disciplines. As public and school libraries speak of joint-use libraries, academic libraries speak of an interdisciplinary approach and this is another area where leadership can be established. The buzzwords related to this concept are "community," "stakeholder," "public-relations," and "internal-marketing" (Bussy and Ewing, 1997).

Much of the literature available on ethnic-minority librarians is from academic libraries and this can be found sprinkled throughout this book. There could be various factors that contribute to this, one of them being the expectation on academic librarians to publish or perish. Weiner (2003) highlights some leadership-related topics and cites papers that focus on these topics. Under *diversity issues*, she refers to papers that focus on women as leaders but has nothing to report on ethnic-minority librarians. Winston (2001) has written many articles that focus on minority librarians in an academic setting and in his article entitled "The Importance of Leadership Diversity: The Relationship between Diversity and Organizational Success in the Academic Environment" he observes that "fostering diversity within organizations goes beyond the fact that it is a good thing to do." Though there is no known direct relationship between diversity and organizational success, organizations that are diverse and successful have managed to be successful by drawing "a wide pool of talent up through their ranks and is [are] opening itself [themselves] to a variety of different views and ideas" (Kuczynski, 1999). In a library situation, a diverse group of librarians will help serve the demographics represented and will help target multicultural users of libraries and promote multicultural collections. But these are not the only reasons libraries should be diverse. Switzer (2008) asks that we stop paying lip-service to the idea of tolerance and commit ourselves to multiculturalism and ethnic diversity. She speaks of academic campuses altering their mission statements to reflect their commitment. She, too, offers a literature review of the subject from 1987.

Leadership programs for ethnic-minority librarians in the US, Canada, the UK and Australia

There are a number of leadership programs available in the US, Canada, the UK and Australia, for all librarians and library staff to attend, but few focus on ethnic-minority librarians.

United States

Association of Research Libraries (ARL) – its Leadership and Career Development Program is an 18-month program that helps mid-career level librarians from diverse groups work towards their leadership roles.

Minnesota Institute – This program is offered once every two years and focuses on ethnic-minority librarians who have been in the profession for less than three years. It has two components: technology training and leadership. This program admits Canadians as well. The director or dean of the participant's library has to recommend the participant for the program.

Spectrum Scholarship – While this is not a leadership workshop, this scholarship encourages applicants from minority groups to apply to library schools. Established in 1997, Spectrum "is ALA's national diversity and recruitment effort designed to address the specific issue of under-representation of critically needed ethnic librarians within the profession while serving as a model for ways to bring attention to larger diversity issues in the future" (ALA, 2011). (http://www.ala.org/Template.cfm?Section=scholarships& template=/ContentManagement/ContentDisplay.cfm& ContentID=55694)

Canada

While there are many leadership programs available in Canada, such as The Northern Exposure to Leadership in Edmonton, The Emerging Leader Program in Calgary, and institution-based leadership programs for academic librarians, there are none that focus on minority librarians.

Australia's Aurora Leadership Program

The Aurora Foundation aims to "develop leadership capacity in the library and information professions in Australia and New Zealand by developing and providing innovative and challenging programs" (Aurora Foundation Limited, 2011, http://www.aurorafoundation.org.au/). The Foundation offers two different classes through the Aurora Institute: Emerging Leaders and the Masterclass in Strategy in Innovation. Emerging Leaders is for those who have been identified as potential leaders by their organization and have two years' experience in a supervisory role. This program is not only for librarians, but also for employees from museums, archives, records management, galleries, etc.

United Kingdom

There are no leadership programs to be found for librarians or ethnic-minority librarians. The only program mentioned on CILIP is the Encompass Toolkit mentioned earlier.

Leadership programs have identified some important factors to help foster leadership in minority librarians. One major factor is networking. At the Minnesota Institute, participants created a listserv and kept in touch about their professional lives. Being part of a network creates more awareness about possibilities in the profession and this awareness is one step towards leadership. Another factor is using inventories to identify the styles and personalities of participants. This helps minorities learn about their current styles and preferences, and when they know where they stand it is easier to identify where they want to go and how to get there. Learning to build new skills is also a factor. Some of the leadership programs have a skills component where the latest multimedia skills are taught. For first generation ethnic-minority librarians coming from various backgrounds this would be a beneficial component in a leadership program.

Statistically speaking

Three different survey questionnaires (see Appendices A to C) were administered electronically to ethnic-minority librarians, deans and directors of libraries, and directors of library schools in the UK, the US, Canada, and Australia. As a result of how the survey was administered (more publicizing points within Canada but a lack of information available from ALILA and CILIP at the time), the results are likely to be skewed. But the purpose of the survey was to take the pulse of what is happening with ethnic-minority librarian leadership issues and is not meant to be exact science. The small sample size available in this study may raise concerns about arriving at conclusions on the immigrant population in leadership fields. The limitations were caused by a lack of responses from library school deans and the lack of availability of information regarding visible minority librarians in each country. While the US has many minority librarian groups such as the Asian Pacific American Librarian Association (APALA), the Black Caucus of the American Library Association, the Chinese American Librarians Association, etc., other countries did not always have such groups to where the survey could be sent (or they couldn't be found). Particularly with Australia, the distribution of the survey mostly depended on ALIA.

The survey ran from (approximately) March 7, 2011 to April 22, 2011 (depending on when it was posted by the library associations). Forty-five ethnic-minority librarians, 20 deans and directors of libraries, and eight library school directors from the UK, the US, Canada, and Australia responded.

Ethnic-minority librarians survey

For Australia, the survey was sent to ALIA for distribution. As there weren't enough responses, individual library email addresses for as many libraries as available (academic, school, college, etc.) were culled from the internet and surveys sent.

For the UK, the best hope was CILIP. When emails reached librarians, one or two of them suggested other email lists (e.g., the Diversity Group e-list) to which to send surveys and surveys were sent to these email addresses as well. As with the Australian libraries, individual library emails to as many libraries as were available via Google were used to send surveys.

For Canada, the survey was sent to the CLA, who distributed to all its members. Survey information was also sent to individual provincial associations.

In the US, the survey was sent to the ALA and all other associations in the US, as listed on the ALA site (e.g., APALA).

Fifty-five per cent of librarians from the US, 35 per cent from Canada, 6 per cent from the UK, and 2 per cent from Australia responded to the survey. Of these, 13 per cent of librarians said their education was from their home country and was therefore not valid. They had to do other courses and build their skills before securing any library positions. The remainder had acquired their library degrees from their new home country.

With regard to the leadership questions (see Appendix A, questions 29 and 30), 40 per cent of the librarians were sure that they were in leadership positions due to the nature of their job. Sixteen per cent of them thought that they were "kind of," "sort of" leaders due to their positions. Thirty-eight per cent were sure that they were not leaders.

With regard to the questions on leaders (see Appendix A, questions 33 and 34), these were the reponses: leaders have a vision, are people oriented, lead by example, lead during change, make decisions based on feedback from others, have knowledge of their work, motivate others, have ideas, initiate ideas, and go beyond what is expected of them. In addition:

- Leaders set direction and pace; managers assign work and schedule time.
- Leaders motivate; managers expect the job to be done.
- Leaders set goals; managers make sure they are accomplished.
- Leaders determine policy; managers administer such policies.
- Leaders can be found at all levels of an organization.
- Managers control.
- Leaders are good managers as well, but unfortunately not all managers are leaders.

With regard to the last question on whether their organization would support them in their leadership aspirations, 62 per cent of the librarians answered "yes." The remainder were not sure and cited budget issues, time constraints in attending workshops, and a lack of opportunities in their current workplace.

Survey for deans and directors of libraries

A link to this survey was sent to the Dean and Associate Dean of the University of Saskatchewan to be distributed to COPPUL (Council of Prairie and Pacific University Libraries) and ACRL members in Canada and the US.

For Australia and the UK, ALIA and CILIP were asked to distribute the survey to all relevant groups. Ten per cent of the responses were from the UK and 5 per cent were from Australia. The remainder (85 per cent) were from Canadian universities. Ten per cent of the responses were from deans of public libraries and 90 per cent were from academic libraries.

When asked about the number of visible minority librarians in their libraries, the average ranged from 4 per cent to 9 per cent. Only one university (in Canada) had 16 per cent visible minority librarians.

When asked about a leadership crisis in their libraries, 25 per cent of the respondents answered with an emphatic "yes." They believed there was a leadership crisis.

Forty-five per cent of all the libraries had their own leadership program that was offered through their Human Resources department, or workshops on management issues, along with staff mentoring and buddy systems. None of them mentioned a program tailored for their own librarians.

Forty-five per cent of deans and directors of libraries in the UK, the US, Canada and Australia recognize non-North American library degrees with some stipulations: either a committee had to approve hiring a non-North American degree holder or the degree had to meet ALA standards.

Figure 5.1   **Libraries and their leadership programs**

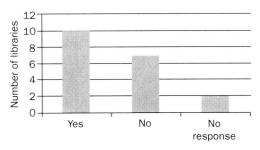

Own leadership program

Figure 5.2   **Libraries with external leadership programs**

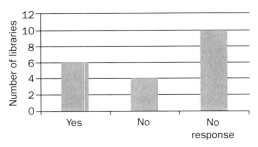

Leadership program from other source

Fifty-five per cent of the respondents replied that they did not have plans to offer cross-cultural leadership programs, 10 per cent were not sure, and the rest did not respond to this question.

Survey for deans and directors of library schools

In Canada and the US, a link was sent to the library schools with contact information on the internet. For Australia and the UK, ALIA and CILIP were asked to distribute the survey to all relevant groups. Unfortunately, there were only 8 respondents (1 from the UK and 7 from the US). Due to the low number of responses, this is not the perfect sample for evidence of what is happening in library schools.

Of those who responded, 5 (62.5 per cent) mentioned leadership as a core course in their library programs. Only 25 per cent have an ethnic-minority focus in their leadership program while others have modules that focus on intercultural communications and mentoring programs for ethnic-minority students that provide leadership support.

As mentioned above, due to the low number of responses, the survey does not give a true indication of what is happening in libraries and library schools in the UK, Canada, the US, and Australia. Librarians in these countries should focus on creating survey questionnaires for their own libraries and library schools to provide a true indication of what is happening with the ethnic minorities in their library communities. As for Canada and Australia, library associations for various minority groups need to be formed. The national library associations in these countries can provide guidance and support to create such ethnic-minority focused library associations that can do more work in the library community to seek, encourage, and train other ethnic minorities from their own ethnic groups to join the library world. All library schools must introduce a leadership course with modules on intercultural leadership issues as a core component of the course. There should also be a module that explains the difference between management and leadership.

Introducing ethnic minorities into libraries and encouraging them to be leaders alongside their local cohorts is not an impractical task. By taking baby steps to create minority library associations that will help in recruiting more students into library schools, by creating a leadership course that integrates the leadership ideas of all cultures, by introducing librarians to different communication styles from different cultures, by making leadership a mandatory course in library schools, by offering intercultural leadership workshops and time for librarians to practice it in their workplace, this aim can definitely be achieved.

References

Achterman, Doug. "21st-Century Literacy Leadership." *School Library Monthly* 26.10 (2010): 31–43.

Acree, Eric Kofi, Sharon K. Epps, Yolanda Gilmore and Charmaine Henriques. "Using Professional Development as a Retention Tool for Underrepresented Academic Librarians." *Journal of Library Administration* 33.1 (2001): 45–61.

All-Party Parliamentary Group on Libraries, Literacy and Information Management. "Report of the Inquiry into the Governance and Leadership of the Public Library Service in England." September 2009. Web. April 13, 2011.

American Library Association. "Spectrum – New Voices, New Vision." 2011. Web. April 28, 2011.

Aurora Foundation Limited. *The Aurora Foundation.* 2011. Web. April 16, 2011.

BBC. "Newham's Libraries Remove Foreign Language Newspapers." May 10, 2011. Web. May 25, 2011.

Berryman, Jennifer. "E-Government: Issues and Implications for Public Libraries." *The Australian Library Journal* 53.4 (2004). Online.

Black, Graham. "The Next Generation of Leaders: Leadership Development Programs for Australian University Library and IT Staff." *EDUCAUSE* (2003): 453–462.

Bundy, Alan. "Promoting Reading to Adults in UK Public Libraries." *Australian Academic and Research Libraries* 30.1 (1999): 65.

Bundy, Alan. "Essential Connections: School and Public Libraries for Lifelong Learning." *The Australian Library Journal* 51.1 (2002): 47–70.

Caidi, Nadia and Danielle Allard. "Social Inclusion of Newcomers to Canada: An Information Problem?" *Library and Information Science Research* 27.3 (2005): 302–324.

Canadian Library Association. "Position Statement on Diversity and Inclusion." 2008. Web. April 17, 2011.

CILIP. "All-Party Parliamentary Group on Libraries, Literacy and Information Management: Report of the Inquiry into the Governance and Leadership of the Public Library Service in England." 2009. Web. April 18, 2011.

Coatney, Sharon. "The Blind Side of Leadership or Seeing it All." *School Library Monthly* 27.2 (2010): 38–40.

Coatney, Sharon. "Leadership for Hard Times." *School Library Monthly* 27.6 (2011): 38–39.

Davies, Steve. "Taking Stock: The Future of our Public Library Service." London: Unison Communications Unit. September 2008. Web. January 12, 2011.

de Bussy, Nigel and Michael Ewing. "The Stakeholder Concept and Public Relations: Tracking the Parallel Evolution of Two Literatures." *Journal of Communication Management* 2.3 (1997): 222–229.

Demos. "Towards a Strategy for Workforce Development: Research and Discussion Report Prepared for Resource." March 2003. Web. April 15, 2011.

Dhanjal, Catherine. "How Technology, Leadership, Commitment and Soft Link Help Turn Schools Around." *Multimedia Information and Technology* 31.2 (2005): 38–39.

Doherty, Gail. "Mentoring GenX for Leadership in the Public Library." *Public Library Quarterly* 25.1–2 (2006): 205–217.

Dow, Mirah J. "School Library Leadership at the University Level." *School Library Monthly* 27.2 (2010): 36–38.

Foster, Rosemary. "Leadership and Secondary School Improvement: Case Studies of Tensions and Possibilities." *International Journal of Leadership in Education* 8.1 (2005): 35–52.

Glegoff, Stuart. "Information Technology in the Virtual Library." *Journal of Library Administration* 32.3 (2001): 61–84.

Hartzell, Gary. "The Principal's Perceptions of School Libraries and Teacher-Librarians." *School Libraries Worldwide* 8.1 (2002): 92–110.

Haycock, Ken. "The Crisis in Canada's School Libraries: The Case for Reform and Re-Investment." Association of Canadian Publishers. Toronto, Canada. 2003. Web. April 15, 2011.

Haycock, Ken. "Connecting British Columbia (Canada) School Libraries and Student Achievement: A Comparison of Higher and Lower Performing Schools with Similar Overall Funding." *School Libraries Worldwide* 17.1 (2011): 37–50.

Hopkins, Dianne M. and Rebecca P. Butler. *The Federal Roles in Support of School Library Media Centers.* Chicago: American Library Association. 1991. Print.

Howland, Joan. "Beyond Recruitment: Retention and Promotion Strategies to Ensure Diversity and Success." *Library Administration and Management* 1 (Winter 1999): 4–13.

Johns, Sara Kelly. "School Librarians Taking the Leadership Challenge." *School Library Monthly* 27.4 (2011): 37–39.

Jones, Darcel. "A Year in the Life of One Emerging Leader." *New Library World* 112.3/4 (2011): 171–177.

Kuczynski, Sherry. "If Diversity, Then Higher the Profits?" *HR Magazine.* December 1999. Online.

Makin, Lynne and Robert Knight. "Senate Inquiry into the Role of Libraries in the Online Environment: Submission from Public Libraries Australia." *Australian Library Journal* 55.1 (2006): 6–11.

Max, Stanley M. "Tory Reaction to the Public Libraries Bill, 1850." *The Journal of Library History* 19.4 (1984): 504–524.

McMenemy, David. "Public Library Closures in England: The Need to Act?" *Library Review* 58.8 (2009): 557–560.

Michie, Joan and Barbara Holton. *Fifty Years of Supporting Children's Learning: A History of Public School Libraries and Federal Legislation from 1953 to 2000.* National Center for Education Statistics. 2005. Web. April 20, 2011.

Mitchell, Pru. "Australia's Professional Excellence Policy: Empowering School Libraries." *School Libraries World Wide* 12.1 (2006): 39–49.

Mullins, John and Margaret Linehan. "The Central Role of Leaders in Public Libraries." *Library Management* 26.37 (2005): 386–396.

Museums Libraries and Archives Council. "Towards a Strategy for Workforce Development: A Research and Discussion Report Prepared for Resource." 2003. Web. April 15, 2011.

Oberg, Dianne. "Issues for the Next Decade." *School Libraries Worldwide* 16.2 (2010): i–iii.

Proctor, Richard and Sylvia Simmons. "Public Library Closures: The Management of Hard Decisions." *Library Management* 21.1 (2000): 25–34.

Riggs, Donald E. "Academic Library Leadership: Observations and Questions." *College and Research Libraries* 60.1 (1998): 6–8.

Riggs, Donald E. "The Crisis and Opportunities in Library Leadership." *Journal of Library Administration* 32.3 (2001): 5–17.

Rooney-Browne, Christine. "Rising to the Challenge." *Library Review* 58.5 (2009): 341–352.

Saunders, Laura. "Librarians as Teacher Leaders: Definitions, Challenges and Approaches." ACRL 2011. Web. April 18, 2011.

Shaw, Lucy. "Encompass Toolkit: Practical Guidance and Advice for Employers in the Library and Information Sector on Introducing Positive Action Schemes." CILIP. 2009. Web. April 18, 2011.

Smith, Daniella. "Making the Case for the Leadership Role of School Librarians in Technology Integration." *Leadership Role for School Librarians* 28.4 (2010): 617–631.

Stewart, Nicola. "Hundreds of Public Libraries Across UK Threatened with Closure." *Wessex Scene.* January 22, 2011. Web. April 18, 2011.

Streatfield, David, Sue Shaper and Simon Rae-Scott. *School Libraries in the UK: A Worthwhile Past, a Difficult Present – and a Transformed Future?* Main Report of the UK National Survey. 2010. Web. April 25, 2011.

Switzer, Anne T. "Redefining Diversity: Creating an Inclusive Academic Library Through Diversity Initiatives." *College and Undergraduate Libraries* 15.3 (2008): 280–300.

Weiner, Sharon Gray. "Leadership of Academic Libraries: A Literature Review." *Education Libraries* 26.2 (2003): 5–18.

Whitmell, Vicky. "Facing the Challenges of an Aging Population: Succession Planning Strategies for Libraries and Information Organization." (N.d.): 1–21. Web. April 15, 2011.

Wilson, Virginia. "Public Libraries in Canada: An Overview." *Library Management* 29.6/7 (2008): 556–570.

Winston, Mark D. "The Importance of Leadership Diversity: The Relationship Between Diversity and Organizational Success in the Academic Environment." *College and Research Libraries* (November 2001): 517–526.

Winston, Mark D. and Teresa Y. Neely. "Leadership Development and Public Libraries." *Public Library Quarterly* 19.3 (2001): 15–32.

6

Conclusion

Abstract: Leadership is a personal journey, a process that requires time and effort not only from the person interested and involved but also from those around him/her in order to create a successful leader. And by those around, I mean the organization and its existing leaders. Existing successful leaders need to identify new leaders from various immigrant populations and train them to be future leaders. Remember the 4As – Acquire, Apply, Assert and Attain/Ascertain.

No community willingly wants to promote bad leaders, but these do exist as well. Good leaders care about their employees or cohorts, sometimes at the expense of themselves. Good leaders focus on a task and lead everyone towards it. They don't create change for the sake of creating change, but only because it will improve the organization in the long run.

Key words: 4As for minority leadership, good leadership, bad leadership

The journey towards leadership is a process. It is personal and has many layers. Unfortunately, there is no checklist to follow to be the right kind of leader. There are only suggestions and examples. Good leaders find their success by trying out a combination of skills and styles and either adapting to or changing the organizational culture.

Leadership is not about proving one's potential or power, but being there for others and envisioning a future for them and leading them towards it. Even with so many books and articles being published on library leadership, librarians are still unsure of how to perfect "leadership." Whether leadership can be perfected at all is a good question to ask. But in the process of learning, practicing, and trying to perfect library leadership, there is room for all to participate. Canada, the US, Australia and the UK cannot call themselves truly multicultural societies if their library leadership fields do not represent their demographics. Leadership is about being inclusive.

The first step to leadership training for ethnic minorities who are first generation immigrants is cross-cultural training that should be attended by their majority cohorts as well. This training should not only be organized by social programs of the state or province, but also by the institutions that hire them. This cross-cultural training can provide much needed insight into their differences and provide intercultural effectiveness (Brislin et al., 2008: 398). These cross-cultural training sessions should not only focus on how things are done "here" but should also talk about how things are different in every culture, and why. Librarians attending this session should be able to come away with an understanding of each other's work behavior patterns, with an understanding that "different" is not bad. The focus of this training should be assimilation, not just socializing.

For ethnic minorities, leadership can be developed in four stages:

1. First stage: *Acquire* – learn new skills, expand knowledge in the subject field, gain experience, understand the nuances of your new culture and the organization's culture and see where you can fit in: the follower stage.

2. Second stage: *Apply* what you learn to your everyday activities. Start small with small projects, committees, and work-related activities. Offer to take minutes at meetings, chair meetings, head a small group on a project, etc. This is the stage when learning happens as one applies learnt skills. Mistakes can and will be made at this stage.

3. Third stage: *Assert* – venture out to do new things, suggest and take on new projects at work, challenge yourself, ask for more challenges, and let others know you are ready for more.

4. Fourth stage: *Attain and Ascertain* – once established, others will trust you and come to ask for help or guidance. Provide direction, make decisions, and identify other potential leaders from the organization.

Figure 6.1   **Four stages of leadership development**

Bad leadership

If there is good leadership there has to be bad leadership as well. Who are the bad leaders? Kanungo and Mendoca wrote, "Our thesis is that organizational leaders are truly effective only when they are motivated by a concern for others, when their actions are invariably guided by the criteria of the benefit to others even if it results in some cost to oneself" (in Ciulla, 2004: 314). Sadistic and autocratic leaders who are motivated for the wrong reasons and lack social or cultural intelligence, or the ability to empathize, might still have followers but will not be the right kind of leaders (think of Hosni Mubarak (Egypt), Muammar Gaddafi (Libya), Zine el-Abidine Ben Ali (Tunisia) and Saddam Hussein (Iraq)). On the other hand, as Ciulla states, Robin Hood-ism is not the right kind of leadership either. Leadership is about balance – a balance of skills, knowledge, styles, adaptability without losing identity, diplomacy and purpose, the ability to balance internal and external forces of the organization, and the ability to balance cultural and personal issues along with all available resources.

Leadership has to be ethical and moral as well. Ethics and morality have to do with not only knowing right from wrong, but with having a social responsibility and having the courage to take on accountability. Some researchers have identified altruism as a quality for leaders. This can be problematic if altruism is interpreted as self-sacrifice. Altruism can be about benevolence and social conscience, about sacrificing time for the benefit of the organization. While some leaders have behaved truly altruistically (think of Martin Luther King and Gandhi), their leadership remains ethical because of the means they followed to achieve their end. So, a leader dying for his cause alone does not make him or her an altruistic leader (think of Hitler) (ibid.: 314–315).

Not all leaders are successful, especially so when they cannot handle crisis situations. Their downfall is caused, among other things, by their lack of sensitivity to the situation and a refusal to take accountability. Tony Hayward, former CEO of the BP oil and energy company, was insensitive when he commented that the oil leak was tiny compared to the vastness of the ocean (Webb, 2010). He did not manage a crisis situation well and his comments did not show that he felt responsible as a company or as an individual for what happened in the gulf.

On the other hand, in 2008, when a listeria outbreak occurred and some lives were lost, Michael McCain, the CEO and President of Maple Leaf products, was talking to the public, taking responsibility and updating people of what Maple Leaf was doing to control the listeria contamination. There was a lot of transparency from Maple Leaf about their upgrades in sanitization procedures, buildings, and protocols, and this established trust with the public in spite of the number of deaths in Canada.

Leadership is not only about success. It is about knowing how to handle crisis situations that are caused by organizational or personal failures.

Ethic-minority librarians! Remember that being a librarian is not just a job that pays. Remember that you are creating a learning society, that you are part of a continuum of learning that spans a lifetime, that leadership in libraries requires continuous planning and challenging of the accepted norms, especially in the rise of electronic collections and technological innovations that libraries aspire to adapt to and use. Good luck!

References

Brislin, Richard W., Brent R. MacNab and Farzana Nayani. "Cross-Cultural Training: Applications and Research." *The Handbook of Cross-Cultural Management Research*. Eds. Peter B. Smith, Mark F. Peterson and David C. Thomas. Thousand Oaks, CA: Sage. 2008. 397–410. Print.

Ciulla, Joanne B. "Ethics and Leadership Effectiveness." *Nature of Leadership*. Eds. John Antonakis, Anna T. Cianciolo and Robert J. Sternberg. London: Sage Publications. 2004. 302–328. Print.

Immen, Wallace. "Lessons in Leadership Spill from BP." *The Globe and Mail*. June 11, 2010. Web. October 12, 2010.

Stevenson, Colin P. *Maple Leaf Case Study: An Example of Crisis Management*. 2008. Web. April 22, 2011.

Webb, Tim. "Tony Hayward on BP Oil Crisis: I'd Have Done Better with an Acting Degree." *The Guardian*. November 9, 2010. Web. November 25, 2010.

Appendix A: questions for ethnic-minority librarians

Personal information

1. Name
2. Age
3. Gender
4. Job title
5. City, Province (State), Country
6. What is your ethnic background?
7. Are you a first generation immigrant?
8. How long have you lived in your new county?
9. If you are not a first generation immigrant but born and raised in Canada (the UK, the US, or Australia), but have visible distinguishing characteristics (skin color, dress code), do you still see yourself as a visible minority? Why or why not?

Educational information

1. What other degrees do you have apart from Masters in Library Science?
2. Where did you get your MLIS from? (Country, State, City)

3. When did you get your MLIS degree? (Year)

4. Does your MLIS meet accreditation standards required by your new country?

5. Where did you get your other degrees from? (Country, State, City)

6. Was your education from your home country valid here or did you have to do other courses/degrees before you got this job?

7. Did you work as a librarian in your home country?

8. Was your librarian experience in your home country valid in Canada (the UK, the US, or Australia) or did you start at the bottom? (I started as a page, then a casual, then went to library school and became a librarian.)

9. Was any of your work experience in your home country taken into account when you applied for your current leadership position?

10. What other challenges have you faced in your endeavor to become a librarian?

Work experience

1. What was your first library job and how long did you work in this position? (Shelver, page, casual)

2. When and what was your first librarian position in Canada (the UK, the US, or Australia)?

3. How long have you been a librarian in Canada (the UK, the US, or Australia)?

4. Name of your organization.

5. Please select the type of library you work in:

    a.   Academic library

    b.   Public library

    c. School library

    d. Special library

6. If the answer is special library, explain what kind of special library.

7. What position do you hold at your library?

8. How long have your worked in this position?

9. What were the circumstances that led you to take this position? (Vacancy came up and you applied and were hired? You were asked to apply for this position? No one else was willing to take this job? Etc.)

10. Are you in a leadership position?

11. Do you consider yourself a leader by virtue of your position? (Make significant decisions, lead employees, etc.)

Your organization

1. To your knowledge, does your organization have a hiring policy that gives priority to hiring ethnic minorities, women, indigenous people, etc?

2. To your knowledge, does your organization have a hiring policy that requires hiring a citizen of their own country first?

Leaders

1. In your opinion, who is a leader?

2. How is a leader different to a manager?

3. If you aspire to be a leader, does your organization provide you with the resources you need (send you to workshops, classes, etc.)?

Appendix B: questions for deans and directors of libraries

1. Name
2. Organization
3. Type of library
   a. Academic
   b. Public
   c. School
   d. Special
   e. Other
   f. If Other, please specify
4. How many librarians work in your organization?
5. How many visible ethnic-minority librarians work in your organization?
6. Does your organization have a hiring policy that gives priority to hiring ethnic minorities, women, indigenous people, etc?
7. Does your organization have a hiring policy that requires hiring a citizen of its own country first?
8. Do you require an MLIS degree that meets accreditation standards for your country before hiring a librarian?
   a. Yes
   b. No

9. Why?

10. Does your organization recognize the credentials of professional librarians from:

    a. Online programs

    b. Distance education programs

    c. Non-North American programs

    d. Other: please specify

11. Do you believe that there is a leadership crisis in libraries in your organization?

    a. Yes

    b. No

12. If yes, in what way?

    a. Did your organization miss great opportunities?

    b. Can you mention a situation that was not handled correctly?

    c. Other: please specify

13. If yes to question 11, what steps are you taking to meet future leadership needs?

14. Are you offering any leadership programs at your organization?

15. What leadership programs does your organization offer? Please elaborate?

16. How long have you been offering them?

    a. For less than a year

    b. For more than a year

    c. For 2–5 years

    d. For more than 5 years

17. If you do not offer leadership programs, do you send your librarians to other leadership programs?

    a. Yes

    b. No

18. If yes to the above question, does the program fit your future needs for leaders for your libraries? How?

19. If you are not currently offering leadership programs, what plans, if any, do you have for the future?

20. Do you have plans to offer a tailored program that suits the needs of your organization and its libraries?

21. If you do offer a leadership program, please tell us about it.

22. Title of the program?

23. Duration of the program?

24. Format of the program (individual assignments, team work, number of days per month, etc.)

25. Does your program cover information on cross-cultural leadership? Please explain.

26. What other kinds of training do your offer to librarians?

27. Do you have any programs that focus on ethnic-minority leadership in libraries?

28. Do you have any plans to offer such a program?

29. Do you have plans to stop offering your current leadership program?

   a. Yes

   b. No

30. If yes, when and why?

31. Are there any other comments you would like to add?

Appendix C: questions for deans and directors of library schools

1. Name of your school

2. Country, City, Province

3. Size of population in the library school?

4. Programs offered (Bachelors, Masters, Ph.D.)?

5. How long have you been offering library programs?

6. Does your library degree meet the accreditation standards required in your country?

7. Do you accept students from other countries into your programs?

8. What are the stipulations for this? (TOEFL, GRE, fee (scholarship offered?))

9. Do you recruit students directly from developing or Third World countries?

   a. Yes

   b. No

10. If yes, what limit (on student numbers) do you have each year?

11. If no, why not? Do you plan to have a quota for students from these countries?

12. How many terms do you offer (starting January term, September term, etc.)?

13. How many students do you recruit each term?

14. What percentage of these students are visible minorities?

15. What percentage of teachers in your library programs are visible minorities?

16. Does your library program cover leadership as a course?

    a. Yes

    b. No

17. If no, do you plan to offer it in the future?

18. If yes, how long have you been offering this course? Why did you start offering it?

19. How many credits is the course worth?

20. Is it a required (core) course?

21. If yes, what is taught in this program?

22. What is the format of this program?

23. Is there a focus on ethnic-minority leadership where ethnic minorities can train to be leaders?

24. In your opinion, what can be done to make it an ethnic-minority focused program on leadership?

Index

CPSIA information can be obtained at www.ICGtesting.com
Printed in the USA
LVOW100347270912

300476LV00001B/2/P

9 781843 346586